Dedication

I dedicate this book

To my wonderful brothers and sisters:

Angel Edward J. Kelly, Jr.

Nancy "Ann" Flannery

Mary A. Daniels

Joseph A. Kelly

I surely am a lucky person to have

Such wonderfulness in the family of

Edward J Kelly and Irene McKeown Kelly

.

We Love Trump!

Don't you? The President was given to the people by God as the answer to our prayers and as a beacon for goodness.

"Millions of Americans." declared Dallas megachurch pastor Robert Jeffries in 2017, "believe the election of President Trump represented God giving us another chance—perhaps our last chance—to truly make America great again. Our job was to elect him once God showed us the way. We thank Our Lord to this day that we did. We love Trump!

Donald Trump got elected because a higher power whispered in the individual ears of millions of Americans. The voice said that together in this election, we could all make a difference, and Donald Trump would become that difference.

The people trusted this self-made Billionaire to do what was best for America and not the bidding of slimy politicians or political donors and hacks. Donald Trump was the only candidate for president who offered Americans a breath of fresh air from the stodgy, bossy, establishment elites in both the Democratic and Republican Parties. In 2020, we need Trump again to defeat the Socialist Democrats and their hate. Our weapon again is Trump. Trump love will win the day.

Trump once defied the status quo of rich donors controlling the government for their personal benefit. Donald Trump to many, including myself is a great gift from God himself.

Donald J. Trump loves America and American traditional values. Just look at the goodness that he instilled into his own children. The corrupt anti-American mainstream press still does not like Trump because he represents normal God-loving and God-fearing Americans and not the fringe sectors of the country. They hate him. He calls them out as the fakes they are. They hate him because he is not controlled by anyone – Dem Party or wimpy swamp-dwelling Republicans. Neither gave Trump an inch and they undermine America by undermining our president. Donald Trump does pay attention to God and Americans are glad that he does. God is guiding our president to a second victory to help him lead America from 2021 through 2024.

We know that the President already turned the economy around once and he is in the process of doing it again—this time while afflicted by the Coronavirus.Trump will overcome all of the country's issues included COVID-19, oppressive taxation; legal and illegal immigrants stealing the best jobs; regulations choking businesses; huge debt and deficits shackling our capital resources; a government Obamacare system that added taxes and made health worse; and corporate offshoring, which created a weaker nation. Joe Biden is ready to continue this because he supported Barack H. Obama's policies which had created the whole mess in the first place.

Additionally, Trump freed our energy supply making us the world's largest energy producer. When Obama was in charge he redistributed wealth from producers to non-producers. He permit a huge, growing, inefficient government to operate. It continually lied, taxed too much and spent more than it had. Our government had become enemy # 1 of the people Mr. Biden wants to bring back those bad times calling them the good old days. A good plan, endorsed by Mr. Trump, along with good leaders such as Donald Trump & Mike Pence is now in place and the plan and the leaders are already saving US from Obama perdition. That's "Why God Gave US Trump!" Now it is up to use to thank god by giving Trump his second term. Amen!

BRIAN W. KELLY

We Love Trump!

Author: Brian W. Kelly
Copyright © 2020 Brian W. Kelly
Publisher/ Editor, Brian P. Kelly

Disclaimer: Though judicious care was taken throughout the writing and the publication of this work that the information contained herein is accurate, there is no expressed or implied warranty that all information in this book is 100% correct. Therefore, neither LETS GO PUBLISH, nor the author accepts liability for any use of this work.

Trademarks: A number of products and names referenced in this book are trade names and trademarks of their respective companies.

Referenced Material*: The information in this book has been obtained through personal and third-party observations, interviews, and copious research. Where unique information has been provided or extracted from other sources, those sources are acknowledged within the text of the book itself or at the end of the chapter in the Sources Section. Thus, there are no formal footnotes nor is there a bibliography section. Any picture that does not have a source was taken from various sites on the Internet with no credit attached. If resource owners would like credit in the next printing, please email publisher.*

Published by: LETS GO PUBLISH!
Publisher & Editor: Brian P. Kelly
Mail Location: P.O. Box 621, Wilkes-Barre, PA
Email: info@letsgopublish.com
Web site www.letsgopublish.com
Library of Congress Copyright Information Pending
Book Cover Design by Michele Thomas, Editing by Brian P. Kelly

ISBN Information: The International Standard Book Number (ISBN) is a unique machine-readable identification number, which marks any book unmistakably. The ISBN is the clear standard in the book industry. 159 countries and territories are officially ISBN members. The Official ISBN for this book is on the outside cover:

978-1-951562-33-5

The price for this work is : **$12.95 USD**

10	9	8	7	6	5	4	3	2	1

Release Date: October 2020

LETS GO

PUBLISH

Acknowledgments:

I appreciate all the help that I have received in putting this book together as well as all of the other 247 books from the past.

My acknowledgments were so large at one time that readers complained that they had to go through too many pages to get to page one.

And, so I put my acknowledgment list online, and it continues to grow. Believe it or not, it now costs about a dollar less to print my books. No kidding!

Thank you and God bless you all for your help. Please check out www.letsgopublish.com to read the latest version of my heartfelt acknowledgments updated for this book.

In this book, I received some extra special help from many fine American patriots including Dennis Grimes, Gerry Rodski, Wily Ky Eyely, Angel Irene McKeown Kelly, Angel Edward Joseph Kelly Sr., Angel Edward Joseph Kelly Jr., Ann Flannery, Angel James Flannery Sr., Mary Daniels, Bill Daniels, Robert Gary Daniels, Angel Sarah Janice Daniels, Angel Punkie Daniels, Joe Kelly, Diane Kelly, Brian P. Kelly, Mike P. Kelly, Katie P. Kelly, Angel Ben Kelly, Budmund (Buddy) Arthur Kelly, and Seamus Arthur McDuff!

Thank you all!

Table of Contents

Preface:

There are many of us who, after crying out for relief for our country for eight years, believe in our hearts that God's answer to America is Donald Trump. The people have learned to love this President as God's gift. It is up to US again to make sure we make the most of God's great gift. Vote for Donald J. Trump for Term # 2.

I knew that I was voting for Donald Trump as soon as he broke through the pack of Republicans and began his showdowns with his real opponent, Hillary Clinton. Joe Biden is the new Hillary Clinton Like many Democrats, I had had enough of Obama and the Clintons, and Vice President Biden. Most Americans feel the same.

My predilection to Trump is much more because of him and not because of Clinton and Biden negatives but the latter are more abundant than any of us would ever believe. Just like we could not trust our country to Hillary Clinton, we cannot trust it to Joe Biden. Donald Trump was a great last man standing in the way of a country ready to go off a big cliff. He saved us and even with COVID, he continues.

At the end of the day, when the dust had settled, and the battle was over, the last man standing won. Donald Trump won the election despite all odds. In many ways he got elected because he was the last man standing between an Obama-like American hell-hole and a return to the Promised Land of our founders. Joe Biden knows the secret of bringing back that Obama-like American hell hole and he promises to bring it back to an unsuspecting public if we let him.

"Millions of Americans," declared Dallas megachurch pastor Robert Jeffries in 2017, "believe the election of President Trump represented God giving us another chance—perhaps our last chance—to truly make America great again. Our job was to elect him once God showed us the way. We thank Our Lord to this day that we did.

What would America be like with Joe Biden in charge?

Many are unaware that Joe Biden has been in two other presidential campaigns in which he won the vice presidency thanks to his promised loyalty to Barack Obama. During their first campaign for the White House, the Obama-Biden ticket "firmly" promised that "no family making less than $250,000 a year would see any form of a tax increase." Within a year America noticed that the Affordable Care Act included a tax increase, aka a tax penalty for failing to purchase health insurance, paid primarily by people earning less than $50,000 annually. Though that levy is gone thanks to Trump, the ACA still includes a poorly implemented tax on medium-size and large employers that don't offer health insurance to most of their workers. I estimate that this penalty, when enforced by Joe Biden will cost low-income families an average of about $700 a year. This includes those whose employers aren't penalized. The penalty's effect on job availability would make its cost felt by a wide swath of workers. No taxes turned out to be the first broadcast of Fake News. Joe Biden promises more.

Obamacare included many other significant taxes that Obama had Biden hid so well and the corrupt press covered up to make them invisible. Even the Congressional Budget Office overlooked their effects when it originally scored the bill 2010. Later CBO had to backtrack. Backtrack is another way of saying the Democrats wee forced to tell the truth because the people demanded it.

Today Mr. Biden takes a similarly veiled approach to advancing the "clean energy revolution and environmental justice" outlined in his platform. Instead of using a carbon tax, which would use market forces to reduce the economic damage but also obviously violate his tax pledge, he would apply the force of regulation. He aims, for example, to eliminate emissions for passenger vehicles, which would make buying a new car thousands of dollars more expensive. As President Trump is apt to explain, regulations are "stealth taxation, especially on the poor." Biden will get any extra dime that you may have.

The And the poor would suffer most under Joe Biden's platform. His plan is to divide U.S. households into five income groups. The regulatory costs of each quintile are estimated as a percentage of each quintile's average income. The costs to the bottom group amount to 15.3% of its total income—representing a burden equal to all the taxes they currently pay. This group would experience part of the cost as lower wages, but the biggest bite would come in diminished purchasing power due to higher prices for energy, cars and other consumer goods. In other words, your purchasing power will go down and the number of dollars you keep will be minimal. Ask Joe Biden about that?

If that weren't enough to convince you that Biden's tax plan would be disastrous for American workers, five independent analyses have concluded that Biden would raise taxes on middle-class Americans:

- The Tax Policy Center concluded his "proposals would increase taxes on average on all income groups"
- The Tax Foundation concluded that Biden would lead to higher taxes "across all income groups"
- The American Enterprise Institute concluded that households at every income level" would see higher taxes
- A Penn Wharton budget model analysis say that taxes would go up across all income levels
- The Committee for A Responsible Federal Budget blasted the plan as a way for taxes to go up across all income levels

Donald Trump saved the US from Hillary and he is the only candidate we have who wants to protect the people from Joe Biden.

Trump defied the status quo of rich donors controlling the government for their personal benefit. Donald Trump to many, including myself is one of the greatest gifts of all-time from God himself.

Trump represents a welcome change from establishment elitist politics. His great ideas for solving the issues facing America today lined up with the thinking of most Americans who were paying attention and who were annoyed at the prior administration.

I am glad that you are reading this book, so you too can understand why Donald Trump was not just a default choice for President. I wrote an essay early in the campaign titled, God gave us Donald Trump. I stood by that thought even after the Democrats continue to add Russian characters into their daily soap opera trying to replay and undo the 2016 election. Dirty Democrat shenanigans are getting old, don't you think?. I have never been more pleased with a vote than my vote for Donald J. Trump. Thank you, Dear Lord.

He is a great man and he is already becoming a great president for you, me, and all those who love America. He knows business and we are already experiencing an enlivened economy. With substantial foreign business experience, he is setting America up as the top dog in the world, and as expected, he is making no apologies.

Trump is a tough American, so we can count on not being pushed around in foreign affairs or delicate negotiations. Our new president as expected, is a winner all the way around. He loves helping all Americans win. He hates to lose and seldom does. America is very happy that we now have someone in charge who believes we can win.

The weaknesses of the Republican Party came out in spades in the primary season and continued as weak-kneed RINOs such as Jeb Bush, John Kasich, Lindsey Graham, John McCain decided to become tools for the Democrats. During the campaign Donald Trump did not even give them lip service.

In his own way, Mr. Trump told them and all the establishment elites where to go. I like that. I suspect God will get them there eventually. These RINOs and their Progressive Marxist friends across the aisle had been destroying America for their own benefit. It took a guy with guts and stamina to beat them. The last man standing stood against them and won a great victory for the people.

Donald Trump first whooped everybody who was anybody in the GOP. He then ran against a person that some call a withered fascist-- Hillary Clinton. There were many Democrats like me who felt that we could not afford a liar in the White House. We were all in for Donald J. Trump. People in my own family who were Democrats for years, switched to Republican so they too could vote for Trump in the PA Primary.

For those who can ignore the media's fake news and outright lies, there is plenty to admire about President Trump. Watching his children in action at the GOP convention and the chemistry within the Trump family, Americans got the full sense of what a fine man and a fine dad he is.

America needs Donald Trump—a businessman and a great negotiator to compete in the world, not somebody like the former president who unfortunately for the country found business as a necessary unpleasant evil. Barack Obama chose to have nothing to do with sound business principles while being in charge of the US economy. Hillary Clinton was ready to be more of the same—a third Term of Obama.

Whether he did or not, the former president gave the impression for years that he had true disdain for America and Americans. It was like he would have loved all Americans to give up their freedoms and become government dependents. I am convinced that he would have liked America to give up its position as #1 in the world to give other countries more of a chance to beat us. Trump is clearly for America and Americans-First and he demonstrated that in his nearly 400 huge campaign rallies. Trump was a Nationalist / Populist running as a Republican because it made business sense to not go third party.

Hillary was more like Obama and Biden -- socialistic and Marxist and she came off even more radical than Obama. For example, Hillary never seemed to be too keen on freedom. She likes her freedom for sure but not yours. She was working on eliminating the Bill of Rights and had already earmarked the # 1 and #2 Amendments of the Constitution for removal.

Yes, we are at the point in our history in which a presidential candidate's position of not being actively opposed to the Bill of Rights was a key selling point for their candidacy.

The GOP today is still full of losers and babies who won't even keep their vows made in the pledge to support the Party's own nominee. No wonder the prior president was treated as an emperor. His sad agenda received no interference from the wimpy GOP. The scaredy-cat RINOS quaked at the sight of Obama. Then they became Never-Trumpers. To me, they are all losers—especially the Bushes, Romney, and Marco Rubio, Billy Kristol and George Will. Trump doesn't quake at anything. In fact, he makes me proud to be an American

I sure hope you enjoy this book and I hope that it inspires you to continue to take action. Our Congress can certainly be more pro-

American and more responsive to the people's needs and not their own. I hope the book in some ways helps you look at things differently.

Our new president has settled in and he is already implementing a host of innovative items on his agenda. He is shedding a dreaded disease at the same time. I hope you digest Trump's entire plan, be willing to adopt it, and add to it your own positive notions for building a better America. And, please do not trust the press to do your thinking for you. And whatever you do, do not trust Joe Biden to create a workable America.

Together, we can help make the US a far better country. We should smile as we accomplished our first and best objective. We elected Donald Trump as our president once. Now, we must support his hard work, elect him for a second term, and give him a Congress without Nancy Pelosi and Chuck Schumer so he can help America even more. Only the voters can get those two out of Trump's way by electing representatives from the Republican Party who will work with the President im keeping America Great Again.

Brian W. Kelly, Author

About the Author

Brian W. Kelly is a retired Assistant Professor in the Business Information Technology (BIT) program at Marywood University, where he also served as the IBM i and midrange systems technical advisor to the IT faculty. Kelly developed and taught many college and professional courses in the IT and business areas. He is also a contributing technical editor to IT Jungle's "The Four Hundred" and "Four Hundred Guru" Newsletters.

A former IBM Senior Systems Engineer, he has an active consultancy in the information technology field, (www.kellyconsulting.com). He is the author of 170 other books and hundreds of articles about IT and topics about America.

Book # 171 was called God Gave US Donald Trump and it has a number of suggestions that when added to Trump's own, that will help Make America Great Again.

Kelly is a frequent speaker at US events such as COMMON, IBM conferences, and other technical conferences and computer user group meetings across the United States. Brian is always ready to accept invitations to speak at political rallies on behalf of conservative and nationalist candidates.

Brian ran for Congress as a conservative Democrat in 2010, took no donations, and shook up the political world in Northeastern PA when he scored 17% of the vote in a three man-race.

Chapter 1 Did God Give America Donald Trump?

Evangelicals Ask God for his help

Deborah Stidom posted this shirt prayer today on facebook.com/WeLovePresidentDonaldJTrump:

"Heavenly father we pray your healing hands be placed over our President & First Lady so that their bodies overcome this awful disease. We thank you."

Many of us who were up late on Thursday October 1 into Friday, got the shocking news that our president who we love and respect, and who we believe we need to fight the forces of evil in our country had been stricken mid-week with covid-19, the dreaded coronavirus. It was a late night for many of us waiting anxiously for any tidbit of news that all was going to be OK.

With medical personnel and Whitehouse personnel putting their own spin on how the president was faring, it was tough to know what was accurate. Getting a glimpse of the president walking to and getting on Marine 1 on Friday and seeing his first hospital tweet were the best reassurances for the public that all was going to be well though the ride along the way might be bumby.

It was reported that a weary Trump, having been stricken by COVID-19, feverish and fatigued from the ordeal, was flown to Walter Reed military hospital Friday night where he is now being given the best care possible. The lasting scoop is that President Trump had been given Remdesivir and he had been injected with an experimental cocktail which was a combination drug while being treated at the White House prior to embarking to the military hospital.

The President had a tough day for sure on Friday beginning from when he learned for sure on Thursday after testing positive. Some said it was a day of being jerked around, after months of leading the country through the pandemic and trying to assure the public that it would not mean doom for America.

After having downplayed the effects of the threat of the virus, and ready to give the American people the benefit of the doubt, rather than pulling a Biden and locking the country down , the president now is reevaluating his own scheduled campaign events. All this just a month before the biggest election in modern times.

The president has now engaged the virus that has killed more than 205,000 Americans and which is hitting others in his orbit as well. We have confidence that he will win his battle because God sent him to us for more than just a four year term .

Saturday was more of the same as the Walter Reed team gave a positive outlook but the White House was more ambivalent cautioning that the next 72 hours would tell us all a lot. The White House earlier had noted that the President was expected to stay just a few days at Walter Reed National Military Medical Center. Again the news was contradictory as other sources suggested the President's condition dictated the change in venue.

One thing that remained true was that President Trump would take advantage of the suite that had been set up by Dr. Ronnie Jackson at the hospital for Trump and his White House team.. It had been previously set up and equipped to allow him to handle his White House official duties in what might be called a remote White House. .

You gotta love this president. He is facing all this in his usual style—bold and brave, while suffering from the COVID. When he walked out of the White House Friday evening, he was wearing a mask to protect his entourage. Positive as always, he gave a big thumbs-up to onlookers, including reporters, but he did not take questions before boarding Marine One.

Face coverings were the order of the day as members of the aircrew, Secret Service agents and his White House staff all wore face coverings to protect themselves from the "covid infected" president onboard the helicopter.

President Trump, always thoughtful of his role as commander in chief, made a parting video before leaving for Walter Reed. In the video the president said: "I think I'm doing very well, but we're going to make sure that things work out. There had been a lot of news talk during the day on Friday about the 25th amendment and the succession of power "Regardless of the speculation, the president opted to remain the full president with all authority intact.

For many, Donald J. Trump, especially with all of the claptrap he had endured from those who could not accept his presidency, remains the hero who beat the Democrats at every turn and every trick,. We will never forget the phony Mueller Report, and the disingenuous impeachment. For those of us scoring at home, the president remains our hero. He beats his adversaries even after they throw their best at him.

My own thinking is that Almighty God is a Trump supporter. I for one am very glad that he (Trump) came along. Aren't you? I am going to stop right now and reprint an email I sent out the other day to remind my friends and relatives about my perception of Mr. Trump before the escalator and before the 2016 election. We are all looking for God to step in again to guide the big Trump ship and of course even before that we pray that God makes our president well soon.

Only those who choose not to see, cannot see what is happening today with all the hate for this man from the left and all the love from the right!. So, today I went back to the Wilkes-Barre Citizen's Voice Newspaper Archives and I found the letter to the editor that I had sent in two months before the 2016 election. I am glad God heard my prayer. I am asking God to hear my prayers again in 2020 along with all the people's prayers as the president's health needs God's touch. And, then of course we need the Lord to bring us another four years of Donald J. Trump.

Perhaps you will enjoy this email as much as I enjoyed rereading it. Those who stand still when they have the chance to act in God's favor often regret their inaction. I am tickled and proud of myself that despite seemingly popular sentiments, I was inspired to write this brief piece and send it in so others could read it.

If I could only open some hearts along the way, perhaps we could diffuse some of the hate from the Dems and the far left. Are they not the same today? After all, we are all Americans and thus we should all be for the best for America.

Here is the note with a few comments [] that I sent:

LETTER TO THE EDITOR / PUBLISHED: SEPTEMBER 11, 2016 WB CITIZENS Voice

There are many billionaires who want things their way on taxes and they figure they will benefit if their lobbyists get to the right politician. Donald Trump is actually running for office as a billionaire. He does not need a job. Yet, he is investing a lot of time in America. He does not need it. But, if he is successful, his kids will grow up in America and he wants it to be the finest country of any possible country ever. Bravo, Donald Trump.

Mr. Trump wants it to be like the America as founded by honest founders. We the people love the president for many reasons, foremost of them is that Donald Trump is intrinsically honest. He may round up on some issues in his favor and like St. Paul, he may boast a bit, but he is not corrupt. He wants his kids to love him and respect him just like you want your kids to think of you.

We are only on Earth for a short time. Why should we not do our best? I love that Donald Trump, a billionaire who needs me like a hole in the head, thinks I matter. He thinks you matter. He thinks America matters. He thinks God matters. He is right on all points. Unlike you and me, he has the means and the opportunity to really show God and his family what a good man he really is.

We had been waiting for you, Mr. Trump, since Ronald Reagan left us. [Now we are waiting for you again—this time to get well so you can resume.] *God gave us Donald Trump.* [I am convinced that it is again up to us to make him our president for a second term. We did not know how bad the Bushes and Mitt Romney were until they went into their recent crying tantrums because they lost. We just know that they were not too good when they had the power].

Donald Trump is bombastic, arrogant when he knows he is right, and he is often inartful in his speech when he is upset. However, he, like my father, is a very good man. I welcome the opportunity to cast my vote for him. I thank God for the opportunity.

Brian W. Kelly

Wilkes-Barre

Chapter 2 The First Corrupt Election Scenario

Is Candidate Trump again destined to win?

Besides God saying it would be like that, there were a lot of reasons that Trump pulled off his victory. It is tough to differentiate direct intervention from the gifts God gave to "The Donald" at birth. Either way, Trump is blessed by God to deliver to the people. God gave him a temporary set back on his way to the 2020 election victory and the President again will endure and emerge as God's emissary post COVID for the next four years from 2021 through 2025..

As a Democrat, when Barack Obama beat "Milk Toast" Mitt Romney in 2008's presidential election, though I voted for Romney, I was not too terribly upset that Obama had won. Like everybody else I knew little about him, but he seemed to be quite eloquent in his speech and did not appear to have a race axe to grind. Boy, was I wrong!

The two-year Senator from Illinois had not distinguished himself in his political career either positively or negatively and being a Community Organizer registered a *who-cares* on the importance scale. Mr. Obama had not extinguished himself, either. He could talk up a storm and he seemed like he would be a man in office who would preside fairly over America. I was not concerned initially. I did wonder, What the heck is a community organizer? Now I know and the definition itself was a harbinger of negative things to come.

For example, my recently deceased cousin Joe, was an executive of a bank that was forced by Community Organizers because of the Community Reinvestment Act to loan to anybody or they might lose their ability to provide loans. That of course would be the death of a bank. The government's imposed low lending standards were a significant component of the 2008 mortgage crisis.

Lenders made millions of loans to borrowers who, under normal market conditions, weren't able to pay them off. These decisions have cost lenders, especially leading financial institutions, tens of billions of dollars. We saw what happened in the sub-prime loan crisis. It was Community Organizers that forced the banks to provide mortgage loans to those who had no chance to pay them back. Nice idea if to was not so costly to America.

Though from my eyes at the time, but I am white, there was no blatant racism problem in the country for Obama to solve, I felt that the Obama presidency would really be post-racial. Like I said, Obama was not my choice but I was encouraged at his idea of a post-racial America. I figured finally the race war of the 1860's was behind us. The Negro slaves won that one with the help of the Union Army as I recall. Obama won this one with the help of the Democratic Party.

I was happy that our go at life at the turn of the 21st^h century was not like when we had those nasty race riots back in the 1960's when I was a kid. Things had gotten lots better in America. I was pleased that with a man, half white and half black, who identified as a "black" president, also understood the white world. With the stuff he got from his mother's side, we could finally put all of the ill-will about race from the past behind us. Surely there would be good times ahead. I really believed that.

My biggest surprise was that a "black man" would be so obviously biased on behalf of the black population. I knew that God had not told him to be that way. I was shocked to find President Obama to be one-sided in favor of blacks. My first glimpse of the President's innate bias was well on display when on July 16, 2009, when Harvard University professor Henry Louis Gates Jr., was arrested at his Cambridge, Massachusetts, home by local police officer Sgt. James Crowley.

The officer had responded to a 9-1-1 caller's report of men breaking and entering the residence. Without giving a blow by blow, the President immediately blamed the police and later had to create a national showcase at the infamous

"Beer Summit," to prove that he, the president was not anti-white and/or anti-police. That was a bad omen for sure. The Beer Summit in retrospect was a farce because in many ways, from my perspective Obama turned out to be a farce.

I soon learned that whites had little chance in the new post-racial Obama presidency. I looked in the mirror and a white guy was staring back at me. From my eyes, race relations were Obama's first failure as president. I quickly learned that I could not trust him to do the right thing for America. I was very disappointed for eight years as from my eyes things in general, not just race, got worse, not better. Yet unlike Hillary Clinton and her coterie, I accepted his presidency and wished him well to the extent our goals were in sync.

After having a sour stomach for eight years, when Hillary Clinton promised four more years of Obama, when she chose to take her turn as president. I knew that I would do whatever I could to help somebody else become president no matter who it might be. I had had my fill. But, I never rioted or suggested that President Obama be impeached.

Donald Trump was not my favorite in the beginning, but he soon became my favorite as I learned that he would not be pushed around by anybody. I like to recall my reaction to Trump when I finally understood him as a *breath of fresh air*. I was beginning to think that the age of reasonable, human presidents had ended with Reagan.

To support him in his candidacy, in addition to sending in some checks and attending rallies, I wrote at least ten books and a number of letters to the editor in support of the

Trump presidency. I gave my books away to anybody who wanted one and brought them to biker rallies such as one held above Scranton, PA in Dalton. The bikers liked my books. The price was surely right.

At this rally sponsored by Chris Cox and the Bikers for Trump, I put a bunch of books out for the taking to help the cause. My most popular Trump for president book was about 240 pages and it was titled *Why Trump?* This book, *"We Love Trump."* Came several books after *God Gave US Donald Trump !!!"* It is one of a number of follow-ups to that very popular book. By the way, my last Trump book from September 2020 is titled, "*Trump Assured 2020 Victory.*" In this book I have a sure way once God makes him better, for the President to assure his reelection. " I am not kidding.

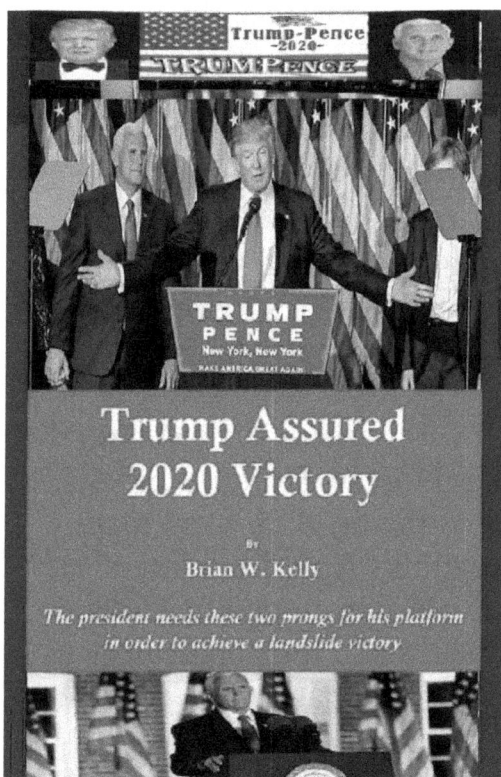

In 2016. to show how I really felt about the Trump candidacy and to help others see things differently than what appeared to be the original and continuing *drive-by-media* thinking, I sent the following letter to the local paper, The Citizens' Voice. I titled it *God gave us Donald Trump.* Yes, it is the same letter I showed you in Chapter 1, but then again, this book is about God and Trump and those of us who love both and I learn something each time I read the letter I sent.

I did not treat the notion of God's role in the election lightly nor do I treat God's role in making the presient well again lightly. This piece is short, so I have included it again below. This time I offer no in-line comments. I really like it and I hope you do too for the second dose!

> There are many billionaires who want things their way on taxes and they figure they will benefit if their lobbyists get to the right politician. Donald Trump is actually running for office as a billionaire. He does not need a job. Yet, he is investing a lot of time in America. He does not need it. But, if he is successful, his kids will grow up in America and he wants it to be the finest country of any possible country ever. Bravo, Donald Trump.

> Mr. Trump wants it to be like the America as founded by honest founders. Donald Trump is intrinsically honest. He may round up on some issues in his favor, but he is not corrupt. He wants his kids to love him and respect him just like you want your kids to think of you.

> We are only on Earth for a short time. Why should we not do our best? I love that Donald Trump, a billionaire who needs me like a hole in the head, thinks I matter. He thinks you matter. He thinks America matters. He thinks God matters. He is right on all points. Unlike you and me, he has the means and the opportunity to really show God and his family what a good man he really is.

We have been waiting for you, Mr. Trump, since Ronald Reagan left us. God gave us Donald Trump.

I am convinced that it is up to us to make him our president. We did not know how bad the Bushes were until they went into their recent crying tantrum because they lost. We just know that they were not too good when they had the power.

Donald Trump is bombastic, arrogant when he knows he is right, and he is often inartful in his speech when he is upset. However, he, like my father, is a very good man. I welcome the opportunity to cast my vote for him. I thank God for the opportunity.

Brian W. Kelly

Wilkes-Barre

After that little piece ran in the Citizens' Voice, nobody had to guess which candidate I was endorsing.

Like many others, I welcomed a change to times in which America was heralded and not put down. I longed for a period in which the Democratic Party and its minions would not parade around the world apologizing for America and Americans.

As I saw Donald Trump, mostly on the US stage, giving his speeches and rallies and talking about making America great again, I was very encouraged. Believing him, was like believing the Gospel, the word of God, according to one of the four evangelists. I still smile each time I wake up and it has been going on since November 8, 2016.

Now I ask God on behalf of all Americans to make our president well again and give him the strength to again fact the evil in our times and prevail. I will help as much as I can.

There is too much hate in America?

We really need Trump Love:

In a book about Trump-Love, I thought I would begin with a little of something that for a long-time was much easier to find than love. I am talking about pure unadulterated Trump Hate. I wrote a book about that topic in November 2019 less than a year ago. Here is the cover and the title:

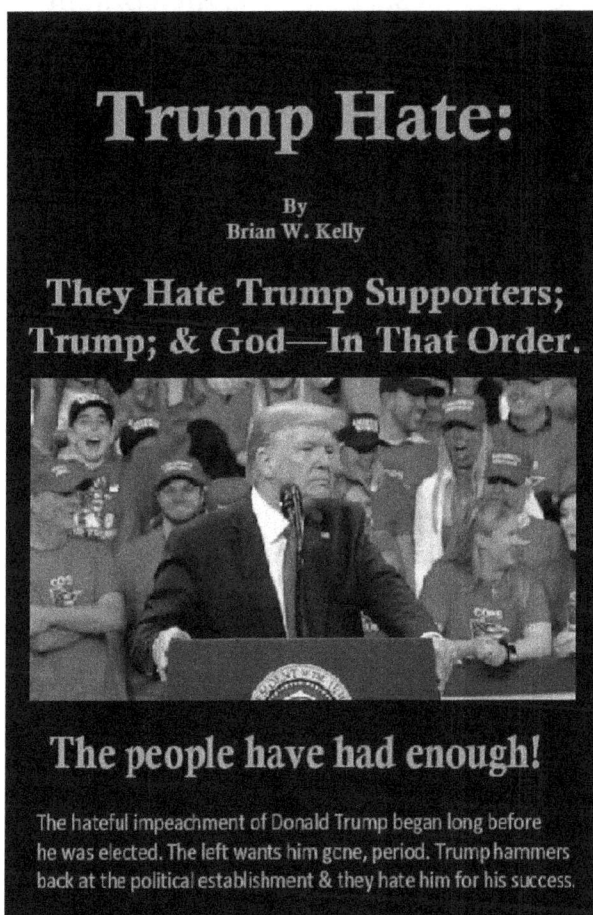

Trump Hate:

By
Brian W. Kelly

They Hate Trump Supporters; Trump; & God—In That Order.

The people have had enough!

The hateful impeachment of Donald Trump began long before he was elected. The left wants him gone, period. Trump hammers back at the political establishment & they hate him for his success.

The well-wish of well-wishes for a save recovery from COVID comes from a former Obama Staffer: "I Hope He Dies!" I am not kidding.

She tweeted and then deleted this short rant after Trump's COVID Diagnosis.

Sweet???

Hard as it is to believe a staff member to former President Barack Obama deleted a tweet on Friday, suggesting that she hopes President Donald Trump dies after he announced that he tested positive for the novel coronavirus. Her name is Zara Rahim. Others did likewise but their wishes are against God's command of love. This young "lady" worked in the Office of Digital Strategy for Obama, as well as serving as the national spokeswoman for Hillary Clinton in her 2016 presidential campaign. She added this preamble:

"It's been against my moral identity to tweet this for the past four years, but, I hope he dies," This was the content of Rahim's since-deleted tweet." What a sweet-heart???

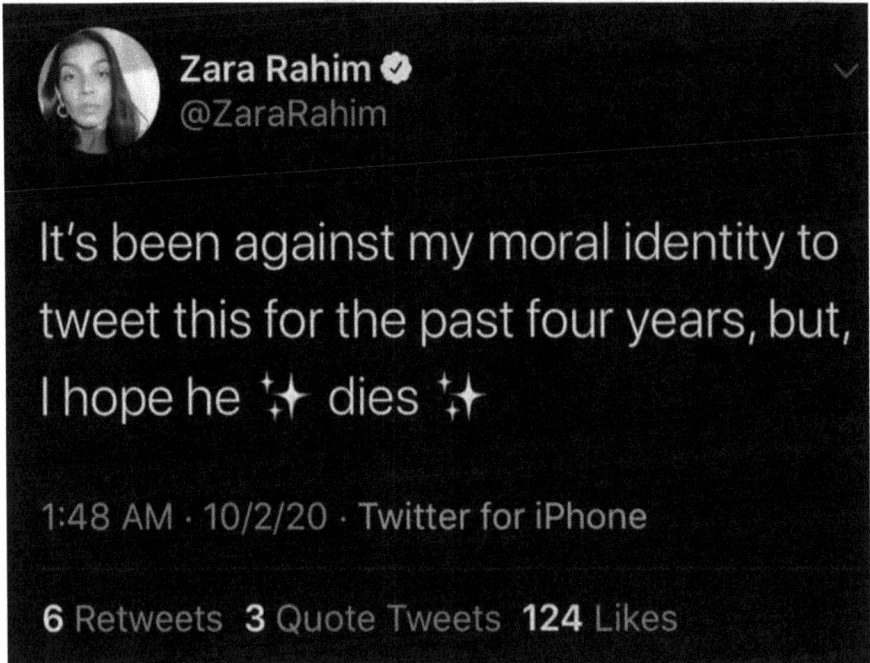

Zara Rahim ✔
@ZaraRahim

It's been against my moral identity to tweet this for the past four years, but, I hope he ✨ dies ✨

1:48 AM · 10/2/20 · Twitter for iPhone

6 Retweets **3** Quote Tweets **124** Likes

That's all she wrote. We're all thankful for that!

Chapter 3 Michael Moore & then Candidate Donald Trump

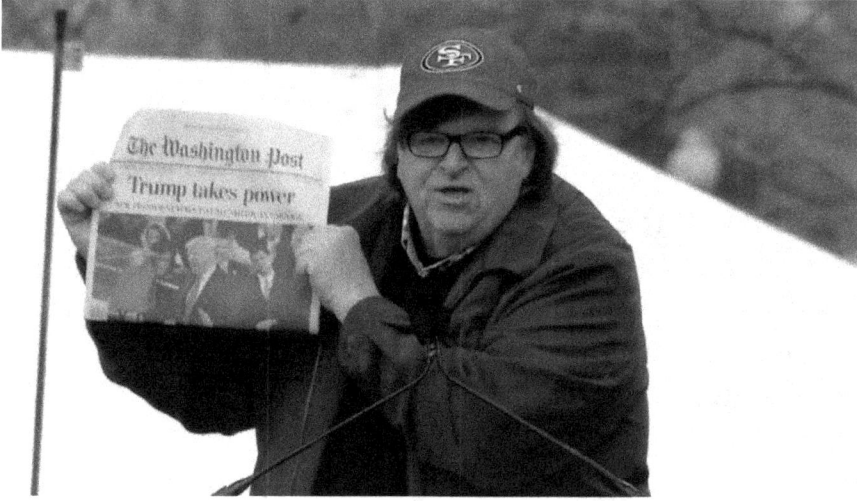

During some time in 2016, I began to believe that Donald Trump might very well become our President of the United States of America. I admit, this caused me some fear. I was scared somewhat of what the dirty Democrats might do to make it not happen. God knows they tried and they are still trying to eliminate Trump. If they could make worse the virus that has the president in recovery mode; if they could wish he be killed by the virus, and have it come true, they would indeed make that wish. That's how nasty they are.

I never in my life saw the dirty politics and corruption that I was seeing in the period preceding the 2016 election. Then again God permitted me to live the next four years. From Seattle, to Portland to Chicago to Atlanta, it is tough to find a policeman who thinks Democrats love America.

From the email survey to the destruction of evidence to the Tarmac meeting with Bill Clinton, etc. etc. etc., the

Democrat controlled FBI forgave her for her crimes, even without the concurrence of the Attorney General. Hillary enjoyed exoneration for her crimes while Donald Trump has literally been persecuted for having beaten her fair and square. Somewhere along the way, American justice had left town.

Hillary would lie and the press would vouch for it. I was ever fearful that the corrupt press would try to slant the opinion of many Americans to favor Mrs. Clinton over the bombastic Trump. That is exactly what they did—as if they were a branch of the Democratic Party instead of the Fourth Estate.

They rooted for the election of another Clinton instead of delivering facts to the people as a real Fourth Estate would do. Trump helped me quickly learn they were not real and their product was not real. Most of the media was engaging in Fake News. The truth was the major victim, even before the American people. It was one of the first identifications of fake news.

At the time, I was unaware that Michael Moore, about whom I have little regard, had concerns just the opposite of mine. His biggest fear was that Donald Trump would become president of the United States. His premonitions came true and I sure hope to see them come true again.

Michael Moore predicted Trump's big win

Who is Michael Moore? Adrian Wooldridge of the Weekly Standard does an accurate job of describing Moore:

THERE ARE MANY THINGS that can be said against Michael Moore. An odd combination of Howard Stern and Paul Krugman, Moore is the king of all left-wing media, from films to books, who specializes in trashing everything that conservative America holds dear. For Moore, businessmen are always trampling on the faces of the poor, Republicans are always the tools of sinister vested interests, and America is always up to no good in the world. But say this for the pudgy auteur, he has his uses as a timesaver at dinner parties in hyper-partisan America. If the woman next to you admires Moore, she probably dated Dean and is now firmly married to Kerry; if she regards Moore as a bilious blowhard, then she is probably going to vote for George W. Bush.

Chapter 4   God Still Knows That Trump Is HIS Best Answer

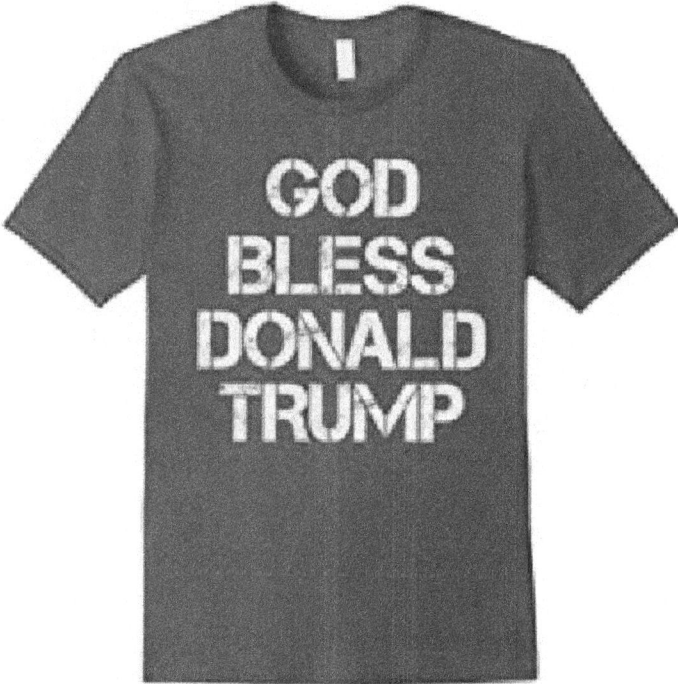

Love or hate?

You either loved Donald Trump when he ran for President in 2016 or you hated him. In many ways such general feelings have not changed. There was no in-between then and there is no in-between now. Having the president infected with COVID-19, the love for Trump is even stronger and Trump appears even more tender than we already know he is. Rudy Giuliani hit it out of the park as he described the Trump public's reaction to the president's illness. He said that "Trump did all he could for the people for three years, and now the people through their prayers and their vigils are doing their best to pay back the president for his care for them and the country."

Now, let me tell you this little heartwarming story. For those who know Trump, they say it is typical of the president. Trump's Chief of staff was with him on Friday October 2 in his suite after the president checked into the hospital . The president saw the crowd outside Walter Reid and the pro-Trump signs. He was touched by the loyalty and the love the people were showing outside the hospital while he is sick.

Wanting to express his gratitude, the President asked Chief of Staff, Mark Meadows to hand out presidential chocolates to this growing group gathered outside the hospital. There was footage on Fox which showed the Trump loyalists outside Walter Reed National Military Medical Center, where Trump is being treated. They wanted to show the president they love him and to show their support for the sick president.

I saw this played out on the Laura Ingraham show on Fox Friday night and it touched me, Laura said that Trump had found out about the group's devotion and had sent Meadows to hand out chocolates, courtesy of the commander-in-chief. How about that?

Trump is no Obama. If you love America, even if you may have trusted Obama, with no good reason, few were ready for four more Obama years with Hillary Clinton as his new name. God protected us

There's no doubt that Donald Trump has said many things that pundits think would be political suicide for any other

Republican candidate. Ironically whenever Trump is Trump, when he makes a tweet or one of his "shocking statements," the pundits often on both the left and the right predict that he's finished because of it.

But, God loves Donald Trump and saves him every time. The pundits are dead wrong every time. Trump appears to be almost totally bulletproof. He's got great spirits watching out for his well-being.

If you do not love Trump and Democrats are mostly in that category, the only thing that might be more perplexing than the psychology of Donald Trump is the psychology of his supporters. In supporters' eyes, "The Donald" can do no wrong. Even Trump himself seems to be astonished by this phenomenon.

Despite this nonpareil about tweets etc., the nasty, corrupt press pays no attention to things that are just plain nice that Trump does all the time. The passing out of chocolates is one of those things. I'll bet that the receivers of the presidential candies keep them forever as souvenirs even if they have sweet tooth's.

If you never figured that out, or if you are now flirting with the new Winfrey on the block to become the popular president then I regret that you, my friend, are a part of the problem, not the solution. It is a problem that America and Americans must solve before this country can ever be great again on a consistent basis. Trump and God got us here, but can Americans handle the success? Will we throw it away on the Winfrey du jour (Hillary or Biden) in the future? Please say "no!"

Can you imagine how successful the anti-American deep state would have been with Mrs. Clinton as president? I thank God, every time I realize that Donald Trump is the President of my United States of America. When she was running on again off again, I wondered what the Oprah's first post-racial address would be like. Since Obama, everything Democrat is about race? It is because Democrats and Joe Biden have stopped dealing with real American issues such as jobs, and real healthcare for the working class.

After three full years and almost a fourth, like many Americans, I still happen to love our President for the right reasons. As I noted in my Chapter 1 editorial, I find him to be a gift from God to the American people in our time of great need. We still need him Lord God. Please hear our prayers to make him well so he can continue your work.

After all the weak, wimpy, wobbly conservative leaders, groomed by establishment elitism, who offered little recognition or solutions for the concerns of the American citizens; Donald J. Trump, my eternal candidate for president and yours if you are like me, has been a deep breath of fresh air. Among the Republican electorate, his approval rating is a chart-topping 90% plus. Hey, I approve, and I am a reluctant Democrat.

Thank you, Donald J. Trump for doing the United States a big favor by taking on corruption in both political parties as well as the media. You are doing just fine and my friends and relatives appreciate your taking a hiatus from your wonderful storybook life and using your time to help us. We sure need it.

Supporters cheer as President Donald Trump speaks in Great Falls, Mont., on July 5. Among Republicans, his job approval rating stands at 88%. PHOTO: JOSHUA ROBERTS/REUTERS

Though some felt when you ran in 2016 that you were not a viable candidate at the beginning, I was not among their ranks. I saw you grow from day one, when you were introduced to the piranha at the first Republican primary debate. You did very well but nobody would acknowledge you because you were and continue to be the biggest threat to all of the establishment elites, in both parties, that has ever existed.

You are especially not liked by the corrupt press because you call them out on their dishonesty. Thank you, President Trump.

You have taken the Republican electorate by storm (now over 90%) and I love watching you climb higher and higher in the polls, though when you ran for office in 2016, Hillary Clinton. was always deemed the favorite by the corrupt media. This was fake news then and there is lots of fake news again with Joe Biden's poll numbers. Now, they have Joe Biden topping the president. It is not true. Trump supporters are a bit cautious of having their homes burned down or their cars keyed and so we are not as ostentatious as the Dems and the rest of the lefties about rubbing it in.

On your way to a great victory in 2016, you also won over many Democrats including a number in my own family— long time progressives who had finally had enough of liberal lies. President Trump, here you are doing it again and when God takes the COVID-19 chains off your back, you will attract even more supporters.

I know Democrats that switched to Republican, so they could vote for you in the PA primary. They are still doing it. They are all very smart people, especially my wonderful sister-in-law, Diane who never gave an inch to Republicans before Trump. She became a Trumpster. It took a while for a lot of Democrats, such as I, to know that today's Democratic leaders are really progressives who care little about the American people and that includes most regular Democrats.

Buried in the disapproval rating are some real conservatives, nationalists, and populists who believed that the elite Republicans who later were identified as the SWAMP and the NEVER-Trumpers, could never be trusted. Some, like the Bushes, we had one time trusted enough to give them governorships and presidencies but God helped us recently understand that the Bush's were always for the elite and they all but lied to all the people about important American issues such as immigration. We did not know it then but wondered why no action on immigration in eight Bush years?

What a disappointment for me and many. The whining Bushes became babies about Trump's rough way of dealing with them as political foes. They are now *Never Trumpers* of the highest order, meaning they have no regard for the American people who voted for them or President Trump. I lost my respect for the Bushes when they exchanged their love of America for selfish retribution.

Along with a number of one-time favorites of conservatives, these guys had always been against conservatives but had lied and played along for political gain. Here is a list of some of the most notorious of these "outlaws" without mentioning the Bushes again. Many, who still hold elected office have gotten quiet or have recanted their negative allegiance.

President Trump has more than proven himself and of course for self-preservation, many came back into the fold. However, there are many more, such as those in the short list below and on the next page who have not come back and many have become dirty Democrats to spite Trump. Why the Democratic Party would even want such people is a conundrum. I put a question mark on some maybes.

Jennifer Rubin
David Frum
Ana Navarro
Bill Kristol
Brit Hume?
Michael Chertoff,

Michael Mukasey
Colin Powell
Tom Ridge,
John Kasich
Mitt Romney
John McCain
Jeff Flake
Joe Scarborough
J.C. Watts
Max Boot,
Steve Schmidt
George Will
Leon Wolf
Glenn Beck?
Stephen Hayes
Etc.

As far as I am concerned, these guys are all either buffoons or goofs. They all have one thing in common. As kids when they took their ball and went home, not a one of them had paid for the ball and none of them were ever paperboys. The scent of privilege wafts in the air as I recite their names.

I read where New York Times columnist declared that the anti-Trump movement is a failure. Brooks lines up with the Never Trumpers and he says that "We have persuaded no one…. We have not hindered him…. We have not dislodged him…. We have not contained him." He went on to suggest that the "Trump's takeover of the Republican Party is complete. Eighty-nine percent of Republicans have a positive impression of the man."

The new Republicans minus guys like George Will who quit the Party over Trump is a party that is almost 100% united for the good of America. Some negative people would say that Trump supporters are all in accord with a supposed Trump agenda of "antipathy toward Muslims, immigrants, atheists, and gays and lesbians, and racial resentment and concerns about discrimination against whites." I think these guys are getting their news from MSNBC. God sure keeps his sunlight from their thoughts. But this is typical of Democrats and the drive-by media. When the truth does not work for them, they conjure up some lies and blend it with some fake news to keep their daily soap opera rolling.

By the way, I wondered what had happened to the cocky know-it-all George Will. He talked his way right out of Fox News right after he left the Republican Party. Donald Trump heard he was gone and fired out a twitter:

"George Will, one of the most overrated political pundits (who lost his way long ago), has left the Republican Party.He's made many bad calls"

I figured Will out a while ago. I had thought his brain got so big that it created head trauma. Instead if you can imagine the Will caricature with an enlarged head—that is really the problem. His head has gotten so big that he has a hard time getting into most rooms and it has impinged on the size of his brain (scrunched it to become a mini brain) to the point that an average Green Giant Pea now exceeds the diameter of his cranium. Who knows how long Will will be able to rant anti-Trump hate sounds from a brain that is less than the size of a pea?

OK, enough of the ad hominem attacks from me. But then again is we think about it, all of the Trump attacks are ad hominem and the press, even the great George Will never complains when Trump is attacked.

God knew the country was at stake

Though the Constitution Party, the Green Party, and the Libertarian Party, and other parties had their own sponsored candidates in the General Election, the importance of the 2016 election was well understood by ordinary citizens. Our country was at stake. It still is for another four years if we let Bien have his way. I expected that many from these parties would vote against the status quo to make America great again. Trump had and still has the only message that resonated with the American people.

I happen to be a lifelong Democrat who has been sick of the Democrat Party for at least the last thirty years. I have similar sentiments for the apologetic corrupt anti-American press. At first it seemed unintentional. Now I see it as part of a plan to indoctrinate the American people into believing that socialism and communism and Marxist principles are better than American values.

For America to remain strong, the Democrats and Hillary Clinton needed to be defeated. They were. Now, the Democrats in Congress and Joe Biden must be defeated. Otherwise the changed world we experience will not be like the America we expect it to be. All citizens were needed and are needed again for us to make this happen. We did it and we must do it again, God helped us all see his light and we did it. God gave us Donald Trump and we must do what need be to keep him in office.

Congratulations are in order for Donald Trump who is still a new guy in a tough political scenario. Despite his lack of funding and lack of support, he was able to overtake all the Republicans, including the whiners and the RINOs and the long-time establishment elites. Trump beat them all. They were ready to take every dollar their donors would give them to buy their support. Trump did not need much but he did put up his own bucks and he outsmarted them all and he won the biggest deal of his life. The president is ready to do it again. It is up to us to make sure it happens again.

On the way to the win, even Michael Moore said that the Convention really helped the Republicans and the Trump Candidacy, which after a year of Never-Trumpers, must still be tracked separately.

How about that great 2016 & 2020 Republican Conventions and the first-class rebuttals to the status quo anti-American speeches during Biden's convention week? It was heartening in 2016 to see the Republican campaign rubbing a little Trump moxie onto the major coronation that was supposed to take place at the end of July in 2016.

The reluctant Hillary endorsement in 2016 by Bernie Sanders and the Debbie Wasserman Schultz firing showed that the Democrats were the Party of chicanery, deceit, and downright cheating. Bernie endorsed Biden in a marriage made in hell but Biden has reneged already on this promises. God always knew it but now all Americans know it too. It is nauseating how far to the dark side of the

Force that Democratic leadership has gone. Why can we not, despite all our searching, find an honest Democratic Leader who really loves America? Joe Biden from Scranton is not that man. How could his brothers and sisters and sons have become millionaires if the chicanery was not more important than honesty?

Was it not a wonderful sight for the Trump family to participate in the two conventions and the campaign for the good of America? It was a pleasure hearing from Melania, Tiffany, Donald Jr., Eric, and Ivanka. What talent! What a family? Even Ronald Reagan had detractors in his family. Why does Trump's family think he is OK? Maybe because he is!

Why does God think Trump is OK? Maybe because he is. But, he surely is not perfect. Who is?

Please allow a digression for a brief discussion of family talent and how families such as the Trump family can do great things together.

America has great potential. It's in there!

My father was one of six Kelly brothers – Martin, Ed, Pat, Joe, Mike, & Phil. They were born from about 1910 to 1925. They were all high-school basketball greats in the 1930's and 1940's. Later in their twenties, the younger five of the brothers played up and down the Wilkes-Barre Wyoming Valley and won their share of many great games against other organized teams. Nobody sat on the bench. There were only five Kelly brothers who played the sport and the bench was always cold.

The Kelly brothers reminded me of the five talent laden Trumps at the conventions. It was overwhelming. There was nobody warming the Trump bench because they were all out winning the game—just like the Kelly boys.

As an American worried about America, I am appreciative for God encouraging the Donald Trump candidacy and for lending the Five Trumps to the people of the United States during his ever so important campaign for America. Again, it is both heartwarming and very refreshing. It is just one of many reasons why Trump won the presidency and why God's favor still rests upon him as he goes for another four years for the people.

We need every one of the Trump soldiers, especially their leader, who thankfully has become our president. He is determined to defeat COVID and regain his strength to serve the people again. There is so much corruption in the deep state and the left. You can see hate-filled biased media speech on all the stations. And, so, Mr. Trump, Mike Pence, and the whole Trump team could not afford to have anybody out of the contest for too long.

The Trump campaign expected bad stuff to continue--low blows, untruths, unkind assaults, and whatever vile actions the establishment elites, the Democrats, and the corrupt media, undeserving of being called the "fourth estate" choose to unleash. The press chose not to represent America but instead represented the lowest of life's== in the Democratic Party and they all loved creating fake news.

So, in the final analysis of why God helped Donald Trump win the presidency, it was because God knew only HE could marshal together all the Trumps, Mike Pence, the Trump campaign team, and we the people at home. God and then Donald Trump needed everybody to continue the fight against the forces of the dark side.

It was very important. Trump not only needed them all, with God's help, he got all the Trumps, Mike Pence, the Trump campaign team, and all of us at home. We continue to this day to fight against the forces of the dark side, the Obama resistance, and the residue of the pre-Barr corrupt Justice Department.

Believers did not believe the fake news. Their purpose was deceit. The truth has always been a foreign notion to the Hillary people. Biden carries the same credo. When Donald Trump won, all Americans won. My sincere thanks to the Trumps for taking on the rot in the Washington DC Swamp area of America to bring America and Americans a big victory.

I still have my smile. Nobody can wipe it away.

Chapter 5 The People and Trump Think Alike

"I love you too. Who said that?" Trump said in a joking manner while pointing to the crowd at a campaign rally. "Who said that?"

It is a new phenomenon and one that almost always brings the President to tears. The crowds have begun chanting at rallies such as during President DonaldTrump's Nevada rally: "We love Trump! We love Trump! We love Trump! We love Trump!" And they need special encouragement to stop their chanting.

Trump supporters really love their president and with good reason. Once he became sick, the love quickly translated into deep concern. The fact is there is only one Donald Trump and more and more of his supporters are realizing that.

You may know that those at Trump rallies have just recently begun to interrupt the rally and instead of screaming "four more years," they scream "We love

Trump!" No matter whether there is speculation in the press that Biden is going to win and Donald Trump's luck is finally running out and his support among Republicans is about to collapse, I don't see any of it.

Heck, when he contracted COVID, those who have come to truly love him for his demeanor and his accomplishments, the people—they kept a vigil outside of Walter Reed Hospital hoping their positive attitudes would help cure the President.

For almost four years, the press has had Trump dead and buried a number of times and each time, they smiled thinking it was the end. But they could not defeat the energizer President. Trump has simply, time and time again taken their dirt and cast it off even though it had begun to look like there was no end in sight.

Even though the media, including Fox's biased Chris Wallace, still cannot get the Charlottsville message right, Trump endures There was never indication for those really watching that the post-Charlottesville polls that claimed President Trump's supporters were on the verge of abandoning him had a modicum of truth to them. Poppycock! Trump supporters truly love the President. Like it or not. The Charlotesville theme of the press is not the truth but it is a dangerous falsehood designed to hurt President Trump. But, the president endures and survives the fake news. And, it infuriated the media. Their lies have no sticky.

Ask yourself, Why do Trump Voters like Trump? Why do they love Trump? It is simply because they consistently approve of the job Mr Trump is doing. It is not what

Trump admirers and voters *are for* that matters. Not hardly. That does not matter. It is all about what they are against. Trump is against the same things and they love him for that. They have a common enemy--the way things were before he came along.

No it is not that a ton of US voters are fervently on the side of Donald Trump, though they surely are - what is more important is that they are adamantly on the opposites side of the culture war that's been brewing in this country since the 1980s. President Reagan was the last president to offer any relief.

Trump is Trump even though nobody has the correct definition of what a Trump actually is. The president has always defied the normal metrics for success. How does a real-estate mogul become a TV star for years with a top show? How does he become the big miffintiff of the beauty pageant set. Trump's voters don't so much support him for what he does. They don't think much about it--but they adore him for what he's against. He's against what they are against and there is plenty to be against and for Trump supporters, it has taken a long time to find the right leader for them.

Donald Trump has had a lot of success in his business life but that is not what holds his base. For example, most don't even know let alone care that "The Donald" as he is euphemistically referred to by the pundits, was forced to sell the Miss Universe Organization which also includes sister scholarship programs Miss USA and Miss Teen USA. Yes, he had to in 2015 after his supposedly incendiary comments about Mexicans and illegal immigration drove away liberal broadcasters NBC and Univision.

Trump had not taken an inventory of his conservative traits at that time . Like a lot of men, in his life the President is known to enjoy the company of beautiful women and he married several along the way who could win the prize in any of his national pageants. His political supporters of today, and the number is growing, do not care that he owned the pageant for nearly two decades, during which time he would have had the opportunity to come into contact with many beauty queens. So what?

Here is what the people really like. Mr Trump is against the political establishment (the media, the Republican and Democrat Parties, political grandees like the Bushes and the Clintons) and change (which encompasses everything you had but fear you are losing).

Donald Trump is seemingly against the same world as the people he serves. It is the world that has taken jobs and sent immigrants to take over America. He is on the right side as far as most Americans are concerned and he does not apologize for it. Americans are tough for the most part and appreciate the fact that the president is not apologizing for America or them or anything which he "owns" or has ever owned. Why should he when he holds that same disdain for the same things as the people he serves and who support him with major allegiance.

Some people say that the culture war that most Americans have not *fallen for*, has its roots way back in the days of the Ronald Reagan moral majority. Reagan too was a Hollywood guy and a good businessman. He was the

President of the Screen Actors' Guild--a union of sorts for actors and Hollywood types. Historians might take us back further to the civil explosions of the 1960s when the "rights wars" were in full swing. Everybody today seems to be for true civil rights. It was a new thing in the 1960's. Most blue collar workers back then were not too keen on riots and they were never keen on people from foreign countries taking American jobs, They are against what Trump is against. There's the affinity.

If you believe America is engaged in a life-or-death battle over its identity, in which the past looks golden and the future looks, well, like it has been painted by the Democratic elites for the elites and the rich, regardless of the impact on blue-collar lives or the middle class, Mr Trump would sound like he's on your side because he is.

If you believe the forces driving the unwelcome changes are the media and immigration, then Mr Trump's 2016 Arizona speech may still be music to your ears. Trump and the people are in accord.

Think of who out there agrees with Trump? Well for starters, it is at least half of Republicans and more than likely because Republicans do not brag about Trump for lots of personal reasons, nonetheless a significant portion— well over 30% of them want all immigrants living in the U.S. illegally to be deported.

There is an even higher percentage of Americans (72 percent) that favor some path to a legal status after a long period of time. The Americans that I know who favor Trump don't like him because of the research by the Pew Research Center, which gives their research a leftist slant and rounds up on the illegal immigrant side. That is exactly what Trump and the people do not want.

Long before Trump entered into the political arena, for example, in the 2013 immigration debate, House Republicans pushed legalization of illegals but not citizenship. After two weeks of flirting with possibly coming around to that House GOP position, Trump has moved firmly to their right in a country that is growing decreasingly white and increasingly Latino.

Latinos to some are surprisingly pro Trump. Not surprising to me because legal Latinos, just like legal Irish make good US citizens. There is a healthy coalition of Republican Latinos in the battleground state of Arizona who believe having Trump for a second term would guarantee their concerns for the country are addressed and conservative social values centered on the economy and faith are protected and maintained.

Latinos do not want illegal immigrants from any country taking their jobs either. They want the opportunity to continue with their personal American Dreams—that is why they came to this country as immigrants. Those who came in the 1990's after the Reagan amnesty were not happy being illegal and they chose to become American citizens. Some run for public office such as a lady who took her oath in 1991 and is now running for a position on the County Board of Supervisors. They worked to become citizens because they love America and they think that is what all immigrants must do.

The liberal press thinks that the Latino support for Trump is counterintuitive considering he rose to power on what

they call *an anti-illegal-immigration platform* in the wake of
porous borders and illegal interlopers working for peanuts
and taking American and Latino jobs. In his famous 2015
Arizona speech that launched his presidential campaign,
Trump referred to a problem with unrestricted crossovers
with no concern for who enters our country. He noted the
truth that America gets too big a share of good people
along with its share of unvetted rapists and drug dealers. It
was true then and still is. Those entering illegally have no
compunction about committing crime. Everybody knows
that their mere entry into the country is against the law.
Americans love Trump for stopping it with the wall.

Many of Trump's Latino supporters in Arizona (the Copper
State,) point to Trump's business-oriented policies, such as
lowering taxes and lifting regulations, as more
consequential actions that, they say, have benefited wages
and employment levels in their communities. This, along
with religious conservatism particularly antiabortion
stances are the reasons they want to see him reelected.

They are fine with being part of the national love affair
with President Trump. Although a majority of the group
had traditionally supported the other party, more Latino
voters believe and say they now find more common ground
with Republican principles, challenging the notion of a
monolithic voting bloc.

A common theme of irritation creates comments such as
this from a middle aged Latino: "It infuriates me that the
government puts me in a box and calls me a Latino or a
Hispanic or minority female...It doesnt work for me,
because I am no different than other Americans in terms of

the things that interest me: to be able to put food on my table, to have a job." Amen sister!

"Most Latinos here, we are all in the same boat, especially the ones coming from Mexico like me. We are luchadores, entrepreneurs, we fight for what we want. We just want to be left alone, and the government to let markets flow." That is why they like Trump.

Latino's like the fact that Trump has a willingness to fight back against the political establishment, the media and the Democratic leadership. It is that refreshing attitude of Trump's that won many over. They say they will vote for Trump again on Nov. 3, 2020.

Some go so far as to say that "it was what we were waiting for, literally for decade." Now that Trump is in place, Latino's are not about to let a man like him go when they know that the excessive bureaucracy of liberal policies gets in the way of the Latino entrepreneurial spirit. Latinos are not interested in jumping through so many hoops and endless paperwork to be able to make a living while Democrats are too willingly and they prefer to help those who don't follow the rules.

Biden is not doing as well as expected. Many Latinos feel the Democratic Party has done little more than pay lip service to Latino voters for years. To characterize a common thought, Democrats tell Latinos that they are their best choice...but when it comes to needing their help, they do not help them. All they want is the vote, all they want is a Latino as a victim.

Trump and his citizen supporters know that the fundamental problem with the immigration system in the US is that it exists to serve the needs of wealthy donors, political activists and powerful, powerful politicians.

Trump calls out these in the selfish class in words such as these: "Let me tell you who it does not serve. It does not serve you, the American people. Doesn't serve you."

Trump says that when politicians talk about immigration reform, they usually mean the following: amnesty, open borders, lower wages. Our president believes that "Immigration reform should mean something else entirely. It should mean improvements to our laws and policies to make life better for American citizens. If we're going to make our immigration system work, then we have to be prepared to talk honestly and without fear about these important and very sensitive issues. For instance, we have to listen to the concerns that working people our forgotten working people have over the record pace of immigration and its impact on their jobs, wages, housing, schools, tax bills and general living conditions."

Trump urges his supporters at his rallies to not give up hope. He urges 'new unity' for once forgotten citizens. It explains why every long minute Trump spends trashing the press for their dishonesty and their cocky fake news, makes perfect political sense. Trump does not have as much support on the coasts but he gains a lot of loyalty from conservatives in the American heartland, and like some members of my family, he motivates a lot of party changes from Democrats who do not like what they see.

His supporters have long believed, with some justification, that just like Trump himself, they too can't get a fair hearing in America's mainstream press, which they see as overwhelmingly coastal and liberal. The deck is stacked against regular people and we all know it. They believe the press has made it next to impossible for them to win elections.

Trump and respect for goodness came out of nowhere and Americans do not want to let go of him. In a recent poll out today by Quinnipiac University, 80% of Republicans say they trust Mr Trump more than the media. That number is growing.

Because of how it was, the people of the US were ready for him when God released Donald J. Trump to become our president. As noted, this first class businessman realized the power of tapping into cultural anger. The people have responded to what they see not what the corrupt media tells them.

On issues of trust, leadership, strength, and values, our president still has the support of a majority of Republicans and a growing share of Democrats who are disgusted with the BLM and ANTIFA organizations as well as what is happening in cities like Portland, Atlanta, Chicago, New York and other Democratically controlled cities. And his base is more solid still.

It looks good for a repeat performance.

Chapter 6 It Is Too Bad the US Does Not Have an Honest Press!

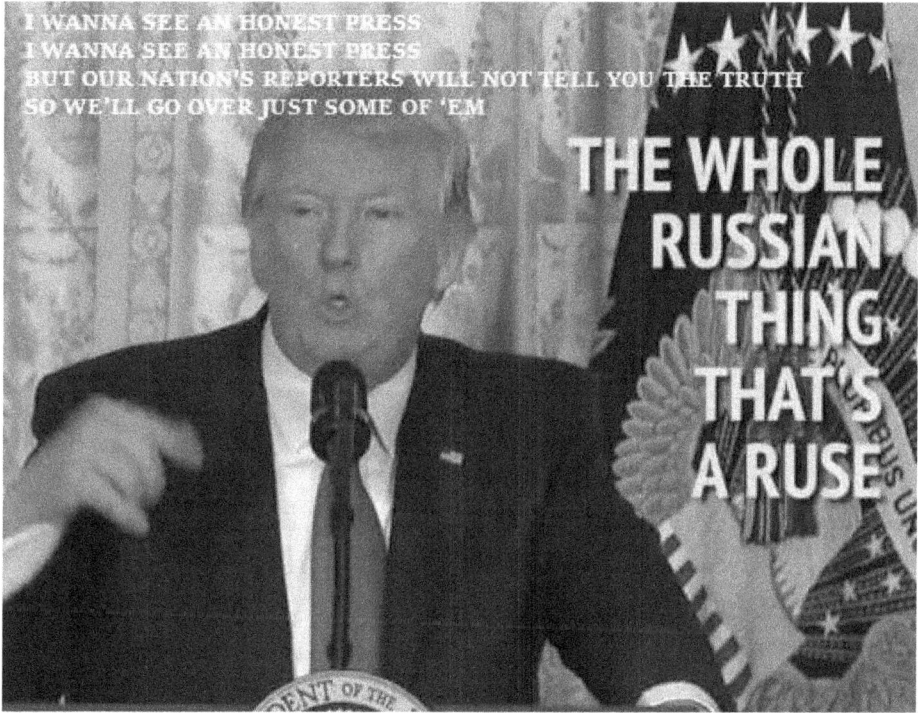

Having fired so many people on the Apprentice, Donald Trump knew the media in the US did not consist of a bunch of choir boys. He found that it was worse than even he imagined. It was as if the Deep State had arisen from the depths of the dismal swamp of Washington just to torment him because Hillary, their favorite, had lost. They have persisted for the last four years in a full alliance with the Democratic Party.

Because he is a smart man, he must have seen the cabal of his political enemies – foremost the men who have led the Federal Bureau of Investigation, the National Security Agency, and the Central Intelligence Agency – as a cryptocracy that was and somehow even with him as the boss, still operates under the cover of the founders' constitutionally established government. Yet, they continue to engage in an immense conspiracy, a dark force seeking to destroy him. Though his supporters do not accept the flummery, there are too many Americans who do.

Trump and the bulk of his supporters and God for sure see the FBI's lawmen as subversive crooks and the CIA's spooks as Nazi stormtroopers. All the worst that he can imagine, they have already done to him and anybody in his campaign or his family that they can get close enough to torment.

He rightfully believes that they have tapped his phones, placed spies in his midst, and sabotaged him since well before his inauguration. And, of course they are all in in cahoots with a corrupt press; and, more dangerously, they were seemingly joined by their love of the "most honest man in the world," Robert S. Mueller III, the FBI director from 2001 to 2013.

Mueller became the special counsel overseeing the criminal investigations of Trump and his cohorts. He is a man who acted as if he had dementia but had been given the power to take apart the Trump presidency and perhaps put him in jail ala Martha Stewart. Mueller who some say was once Republican, hired all Democrats to bring Trump down. Yet, in the end, he could not get the goods on the president but tormented him and his team nonetheless.

While I wake up smiling that the President still is on duty, working on my behalf, he wakes up knowing there are those who would love to eliminate him from earth if they could. I am so glad that Donald Trump is a smart and strong man. So are many in America and with his recent illness the love for Trump is pouring in.

Four years ago, the chant was "Lock her up!" but recently, because the people now know the president, they have actually stunned Trump With Fervent "We Love You" Chant At Rallies in NC & MI. Watching these rallies, even before he was infected with COVID, the president Trump appears to be caught off guard as the crowd chants "We Love You!" It is amazing, He appears humbled and sincerely appreciative of the gesture. This could be one of the best rally moments ever. I would say so.

Do we have a Fourth Estate today?

The intellectuals of the 18th and 19th centuries, especially Edmund Burke, gave us the notion of Fourth Estate (the press and all other media) as a civil watchdog to keep an eye on those in power. It is very clear from the writing of Thomas Paine and others, who pointed out and also acted upon the idea, that we may have just cause to overthrow the state if it is seen to be no longer acting in our interests. This is not trivial. For its own reasons, the press in the US has abdicated its role as the Fourth Estate. The natives are not yet restless enough to overthrow the government but some think we were pretty close during the Obama Times.

Not everybody knows that the founders were not thinking "hunting," when they explicitly added the Second Amendment to the Bill of Right. Their reasoning was and still is what really drives Americans to actively defend the second amendment. Though hunting with rifles is important, it is not hunting that is the root cause of the drive by patriotic Americans to protect the founders' intention of second Amendment.

There is the possibility and perhaps there is even a likelihood that at some time in the future, scoundrels would take over the government and would need to be dealt a blow that only an armed citizenry could deliver. Has that already happened? We may be inclined to ask this when we see all the formal dishonesty and deceit in the media and in the Democratic Party, especially the far left.

The media today from all we can see, would be on the side of the scoundrels so it may not be as easy to defend as the founder's envisioned. In their worst day scenario, the founders would never have envisioned the Fourth Estate going bad on America. Finding that the very scoundrels who have been driving our country to perdition are also trying as hard as they can to take our guns away, make this notion ever more frightening and real. This is just another of many reasons why Trump was elected.

Today, governments such as ours that make the claim to be acting in the "public interest" must face daily scrutiny of their actions. This is a necessary duty of an alert public in a democratic republic. The government must be called to account when overstepping the bounds of what citizens will support, or when taking actions that are clearly not in our interests. Today the press, unfortunately is in deep cahoots with the Democratic Party. It is as if the organizations merged at some time in the last five years. r

There was a time when the public could rely on journalists and the news media to do the Fourth Estate stuff on our behalf. This separation between the people and the state becomes more important when the economic interests of the powerful establishment elites so frequently dominate society.

In our modern world, the interest of "the nation," can be deduced to be no more than the collective interest of those who wield political and economic power. That of course in 2016 gave rise to the silent revolution that put Donald Trump in office. We continue to experience this today as residue of the prior administration operating as the deep state as they have been interfering with a full and clean transition of power. Some worry that the voice of the people has been all but snuffed out by the powerful. The people are mad as hell and are not going to take it anymore. Donald Trump's presidency is proof of that.

Today, the state is the executive branch of the ruling class. And, more and more these "rulers," have stopped believing in a government of the people, by the people, and for the people. Former president Obama claimed to have been a Constitutional Law Professor. Yet he attacked the Constitution daily by taking many unlawful actions of which most are aware.

Remnants of his administration continue their attempts to assault The Constitution, the one document that gives the people all of the rights in America. This is another big reason why Trump got elected. We the people are no longer willing to settle for a government of the government, by the government and for the government. Unfortunately, for eight years before Trump, it would have been difficult to tell. That is why those who follow what's happening expect the people to rally again for Trump for another four years.

The news media – as the tribune of "the people" – has a major role as the Fourth Estate to constantly be on guard and alert to actions of the state, particularly when those actions may harm the interests of citizens. In recent years, the Fourth Estate has mostly been absent, serving as a wing of the Democratic Party. Since the onset of the Trump Administration, the Fourth Estate has actually disappeared. President Trump nonetheless gets his messages out by talking on social media directly to the people. He will do so with or without an honest press.

It would be nice if the press and the corrupt Democratic Party were not joined at the hip today. If it were not for a portion of Fox News and National Radio programs, and of course for the President's Tweets, and shows such as Rush Limbaugh, Sean Hannity, Laura Ingraham, and Michael Savage, there would be no truth available in America today. Though the Fourth Estate for over 200 years was vital to the interests of American citizens, somehow, we have been able to do fine without them from Trump's inauguration in 2017 and we will continue as long as the Fourth Estate sees fit to abandon the people.

Because our foes are Donald Trump's foes, while the Trump and Pence campaign gained momentum before its victory in November 2016, emboldened Trump haters on both sides of the political spectrum – the Bush supporters and Clinton Supporters—got more vicious. In response, the people of America, aligned with the values brought forth in the Trump campaign fought back because there simply was no room to lose this battle against the dark forces, who for their own selfish interests were determined to keep the country weak. And so, we have yet another reason for the Trump victory.

From the moment the TEA Party was born, and even now that the TEA is not as visible, Americans have been unwilling to take it anymore. While wishing and hoping that the official establishment would find its way and begin to represent the people in the way that got them elected, Donald Trump gave us a true hope that we could do it without the establishment.

Trump helped Americans once again feel that America is God's Country or as President Reagan would call it, *a Shining City upon a Hill*. The times from the recent past when there were glimmers from empty promises that were never fulfilled are over. Americans demanded and got a responsive government as promised by Donald Trump and Mike Pence. Yes, this too is a big reason why Trump got elected and why the process will be repeated in 2020.

Too bad our Congress has not gotten that full message yet. There was some weeping and gnashing of teeth as RINOS Never Trumpers take off for home after the 2018 elections. It is not nice to withhold support from President Trump. Unfortunately, it helped the Democrats take over the House. We saw the disregard Pelosi's House house had for most of America. We must send Nancy and her gang packing in 2020.

It is the reason why so many of us joined with Donald Trump and the Trump family and the Trump campaign to get rid of the wretched establishment swamp. With

Trump's clear and refreshing messages about making America great again, we became his loyal supporters. We elected Trump because we trust him.

We continue to believe that Donald Trump will keep his word as have presidents of the past such as John Fitzgerald Kennedy and Ronald Wilson Reagan. I can still see the Five Trumps playing on the first team at both conventions, all believing in the Trump candidacy and in America and Americans. When it was America's turn to believe in the whole Trump family, we elected Donald J. Trump as our president. We are still smiling.

We the people have simply gotten sick of everything being for the Republican big shots. We are tired of the establishment elites such as the George Bushes, Jeb Bush, Carl Rove, Brit Hume, the US Chamber of Commerce, and the many donors who think they can buy America simply by buying its weak, whiny, and wimpy politicians.

Meanwhile we see the Democrats of today brewing up one falsehood after another for the corrupt press to spread on an unwary accepting public that is too full of low information voters. Their objective right from the beginning has been to finish off the Trump team by telling enough lies that the people would finally believe them and acquiesce. They underrated those of us that see through their chicanery.

This will not happen this time! Democrat constituents saw the vile of the dishonest Democratic Party leaders and Hillary Clinton when they destroyed Bernie Sanders in a conspiracy of lies and double-dealing. More and more Democrats left the Party to vote for Donald Trump in primaries across the country and then, they stuck with Trump as the only salvation for the country right through the general election to today. That's why Trump got elected and why he will be inaugurated again in 2021. For now, we have to find some fresh honest Republicans to replace those Democrats in Congress as well as a number of stodgy swamp Republicans.

A small establishment elite had been running the Republican Party for far too long. They rigged the game against the people and were accustomed to things going their way. The beauty of the Trump election was that these RINOs got caught flat-footed when their old tricks and their "ram it quietly down their throats," tactics simply did not work on Americans this time.

Why? It was because Donald Trump, the antitheses of the establishment had already entered the arena, and he proceeded to knock the elites over one by one. Along the way he convinced the majority of Americans in a majority of the states that he was the real deal. And, so, we elected him President. The Trump honesty continues to be refreshing despite him being under attack by the most dishonest political class in US history. When he recovers from COVID soon, he will again lead America towards a better life for all. V

The rise of Trump was nothing less than a tidal wave. In their deluded minds, the establishment actually thought they could steal the nomination from Donald Trump and that their strategy would work just the same as it did against Ron Paul in 2012. But Trump has a constituency, which includes you and yours truly. that would not stand for it. And, so, he got elected in 2016 as a people's favorite.

I am reminded of Japanese Naval Marshal General Isoroku Yamamoto who, after Pearl Harbor confessed: "I fear all we have done is to awaken a sleeping giant and filled him with a terrible resolve." The attempts of the establishment elites to derail the Trump Campaign were thwarted by a fed-up public. We wanted Trump, period! We the public had gotten very sick of Republican broken promises. We lost trust in the Party elite leaders and the donors who no longer care about the people. And, with firm resolve we won the presidential election for Donald Trump. We know we need to stock the Congress with Trump supporters in 2020 and that will happen.

Yes, Donald Trump did manage to awaken the silent majority of Americans who previously either did not care or simply did not bother to vote. Some in the past just shrugged their shoulders and accepted that the system was rigged and that all of the little men in the world—all of us insignificant citizens of America, could not make an impact under any circumstances. Trump is the difference. The people rose up and are taking our power back. That is why Trump got elected and why he will be back for four more in 2021.

Trump has always been for the non-establishment brand of citizen, who simply depends on honest representatives to keep our democratic republic operating smoothly. He is the perfect alternative to candidates who do the bidding of Bush's and Clintons and their ilk, who somehow have become richer and richer while the ordinary people have become poorer and poorer. Donald J. Trump became the perfect alternative for leaders who had permitted America herself to be turned into a debt-ridden shadow of its once great self.

Unfortunately, because of elitist propaganda from both Republicans and Democrat members of the establishment, in full cahoots with the corrupt main stream media, the fourth estate, full of journalists that have forgotten American History, Americans chose a quiet revolt. We hear it all and are disgusted and we are lined up against those still willing and eager to put forth their hatred against Donald Trump like as if it is the common opinion. We voted for Donald Trump against all those lies and the daily soap opera and we are ready to support him against all odds.

Chapter 7 What is a Donald Trump?

Heading for Walter Reed Hospital for Treatment

Right or wrong about Trump?

I have such a wonderful group of email friends that I never feel alone. Over the years, we of like mind have gotten to know each other well so that rather than just ideological arguments which go no place, we send each other emails that help substantiate the conservative position. I, of course am a conservative Democrat like JFK, and more than likely I am the only Democrat on their email list.

If you, like me are a Trump guy, even if you cannot come up with a catch-phrase to tell it all in a quick sound bite, think of this next email as a continuous sound bite designed to tell us all we need about *What is a Donald Trump*.

Like other emails that I have used to help us all know "How God selected and supported Donald Trump in 2016," this one is also right on the mark. I am going to have to find another for 2020.

I did not write any of this email unless it is a comment in brackets []. It was sent early in 2016. With people thinking like this, it is easier to see how, with the help of God, Trump pulled off his great victory. I hope you like it. It is just what the doctor ordered for a Trump supporter's smile.

Sent: 1/28/2016 10:06:38 A.M. Eastern Standard Time
Subj: OMG- a 'Keeper'- "What Is Donald Trump?" (So well written & FUNNY too!)

I did a search on 'truthorfiction.com' (I don't trust Snopes.) for the author Don Frederick & there's one by that name who writes for Bloomberg, but I could not find this particular column. --- It's great, whether he wrote it or not.

The author (Don Frederick) is the political correspondent for Bloomberg and he wrote extensively about Trump even before he was elected, and he did it with facts and more facts.

Here goes:

"Who is Donald Trump?" The better question may be, "What is Donald Trump?"

The answer: A giant middle finger from average Americans to the political and media establishment.

Some Trump supporters are like the 60's white girls who dated black guys just to annoy their parents. But most Trump supporters have simply had it with the Demosocialists and the "Republicans in Name Only."

They know there isn't a dime's worth of difference between Hillary Rodham and Jeb Bush, and only a few cents worth between Rodham and the other GOP candidates. [There is no difference between Hillary and Joe Biden, especially Sleepy Joe Biden.]

Ben Carson is not an "establishment" candidate, but the Clinton machine would pulverize Carson, and the somewhat rebellious Ted

Cruz will (justifiably so) be tied up with natural born citizen lawsuits (as might Marco Rubio).

The Trump supporters figure they may as well have some fun tossing Molotov cocktails at Wall Street and Georgetown while they watch the nation collapse. Besides, lightning might strike, Trump might get elected, and he might actually fix a few things. Stranger things have happened. (The nation elected a Marxist in 2008 and Bruce Jenner now wears designer dresses.)

Millions of conservatives are justifiably furious. They gave the Republicans control of the House in 2010 and control of the Senate in 2014 and have seen them govern no differently than Nancy Pelosi and Harry Reid. Yet those same voters are supposed to trust the GOP in 2016? Why? Trump did not come from out of nowhere. His candidacy was created by the last six years of Republican failures.

No reasonable person can believe that any of the establishment candidates will slash federal spending, rein in the Federal Reserve, cut burdensome business regulations, reform the tax code, or eliminate useless federal departments (the Departments of Education, Housing and Urban Development, Energy, etc.). Even Ronald Reagan was unable to eliminate the Department of Education. (Of course, getting shot at tends to make a person less of a risk-taker.)

No reasonable person can believe that any of the nation's major problems will be solved by Rodham, Bush, and the other dishers of donkey fazoo now eagerly eating corn in Iowa and pancakes in New Hampshire.

Many Americans, and especially Trump supporters, have had it with:

- ✓ Anyone named Bush
- ✓ Anyone named Clinton
- ✓ Anyone named Biden
- ✓ Anyone who's held political office
- ✓ Political correctness
- ✓ Illegal immigration
- ✓ Massive unemployment
- ✓ Phony "official" unemployment and inflation figures

- ✓ Welfare waste and fraud
- ✓ People faking disabilities to go on the dole
- ✓ VA waiting lists
- ✓ TSA airport groping
- ✓ ObamaCare
- ✓ The Federal Reserve's money-printing schemes
- ✓ Wall Street crooks like Jon Corzine
- ✓ Michelle Obama's vacations
- ✓ Michelle Obama's food police
- ✓ Barack Obama's golf
- ✓ Barack Obama's arrogant and condescending lectures
- ✓ Barack Obama's criticism/hatred of America
- ✓ Valerie Jarrett
- ✓ "Holiday trees"
- ✓ Hollywood hypocrites
- ✓ Global warming nonsense
- ✓ Cop killers
- ✓ Gun confiscation threats
- ✓ Stagnant wages
- ✓ Chevy Volts
- ✓ Clock boy
- ✓ Pajama boy
- ✓ Mattress girl
- ✓ Boys in girls' bathrooms
- ✓ Whiny, spoiled college students who can't even place the Civil War in the correct century

...and that's just the short list.

Trump supporters believe that no Democrat wants to address these issues, and that few Republicans have the courage to address these issues. They certainly know that none of the establishment candidates are better than barely listening to them, and Trump is their way of saying, "Screw you, Hillary Rodham Rove Bush!"

The more the talking head political pundits insult the Trump supporters, the more supporters he gains. (The only pundits who seem to understand what is going on are Democrats Doug Schoen and Pat Caddell and Republican John LeBoutillier. All the others argue that the voters will eventually "come to their senses" and support an establishment candidate.)

But America does not need a tune-up at the same old garage. It needs a new engine installed by experts--and neither Rodham nor Bush are mechanics with the skills or experience to install it. Hillary Rodham is not a mechanic; she merely manages a garage her philandering husband abandoned. Jeb Bush is not a mechanic; he merely inherited a garage. [Joe Biden is in the game in 2020 because his fallback is to get a job at a mattress distributor in the sleepy lane]

Granted, Trump is also not a mechanic, but he knows where to find the best ones to work in his garage. He won't hire his brother-in-law or someone to whom he owes a favor; he will hire someone who lives and breathes cars.

"How dare they revolt!" the "elites" are bellowing. Well, the citizens are daring to revolt, and the RINOs had better get used to it. "But Trump will hand the election to Clinton!" That is what the Karl Rove-types want people to believe, just as the leftist media eagerly shoved "Maverick" McCain down GOP throats in 2008--knowing he would lose to Obama.

But even if Trump lost and Rodham won, she would not have been dramatically different than Bush or most of his fellow candidates. They would have been be nothing more than caretakers, not working to restore America's greatness but merely presiding over the collapse of a massively in-debt nation.

A nation can perhaps survive open borders; a nation can perhaps survive a generous welfare system. But no nation can survive both-- and there is little evidence that the establishment candidates of either party understood that. The United States could not forever continue on the path it was on. At some point it would be destroyed by its debt.

Yes, Trump speaks like a bull wandering through a china shop, but the truth is that the borders did need to be sealed; we cannot afford to feed, house, and clothe 200,000 Syrian immigrants for decades (even if we get inordinately lucky and none of them are ISIS infiltrators or

Syed Farook wannabes); the world is at war with radical Islamists; all the world's glaciers are not melting; and Rosie O'Donnell is a fat pig.

Is Trump the perfect candidate? Of course not. Neither was Ronald Reagan. But unless we close our borders and restrict immigration, all the other issues are irrelevant. One terrorist blowing up a bridge or a tunnel could kill thousands. One jihadist poisoning a city's water supply could kill tens of thousands. One electromagnetic pulse attack from a single Iranian nuclear device could kill tens of millions. Faced with those possibilities, most Americans probably don't care that Trump relied on eminent domain to grab up a final quarter acre of property for a hotel, or that he boils the blood of the Muslim Brotherhood thugs running the Council on American-Islamic Relations.

While Attorney General Loretta Lynch's greatest fear was that someone might give a Muslim a dirty look, most Americans were more worried about being gunned down at a shopping mall by a crazed lunatic who treats his prayer mat better than his three wives and who thinks 72 virgins are waiting for him in paradise.

The establishment were frightened to death in 2016 that Trump would win, but not because they believed he would harm the nation. BTW, they are afraid again in 2020 for the same reason. They are afraid he will upset their taxpayer-subsidized apple carts. While Obama threatened to veto legislation that spent too little, they worry that Trump will veto legislation that spends too much.

Back when, You could be certain that if an establishment candidate won in November 2016, his or her cabinet positions would be filled with the same people we've seen before. The washed-up has-beens of the Clinton and Bush administrations will be back in charge. The hacks from Goldman Sachs will continue to call the shots. Whether it is Bush's Karl Rove or Clinton's John Podesta who makes the decisions in the White House will matter little. If the establishment wins, America loses.

Don Fredrick
-- End of email --

Chapter 8 Trump Worked Hard to Become President

Wants to be best president ever

I waited a little bit, until this chapter, before I told you in Donald John Trump's words Why God helped Trump get elected. It is no secret. Trump got elected because he is Trump. Nobody else could have pulled it off. Nobody else! He told us he would be our next president and like many others, I believed him.

Seventeen Republicans and four Democrats for sure did not believe him. The low information crowd in America did not believe him either but then again, they got all their information from the Democratic Party and the low-ratings, corrupt, fake-news media. Most never heard the truth once during Trump's 1.5 year campaign for office.

Yet, Trump told us all, believers and non-believers alike that he would be our next president, how he would become our president, and why he would be our next president. He first told it to us all on June 16, 2015, and he did not waiver off point for over a year and a half. Then he walked away with the presidency despite the polls and despite the lies of Democratic leaders who are still shell-shocked.

Trump struck a chord with the American people. The Obama administration was one lie after another. Eventually all these little time bombs went off and those of us paying attention knew we needed something big to get America back on track. Donald Trump supersized his campaign and he promised to supersize America when elected. He promised quite simply to Make America Great Again. His message said it all. It was clear and energizing and it made Americans feel good that somebody who cared was finally going to run America.

You can take any of Trump's 186 primary rallies or his 137 general election rallies across the United States in 2016 and his message was the same as it was on June 16, 2015 when he walked down the escalator at Trump Towers with Melania to get in the presidential foray. Make America Great Again with facts and plans to match. 2021 will be another great Trump beginning.

Trump's Trip Down the Escalator

Donald Trump's Presidential Announcement

June 16, 2015

Think about a guy, mostly unscripted talking from the heart to the American people. Then, as you go back and read his speech, along with all Trump supporters, you too will know Why God helped Trump get Elected!

Here are some tidbits from his announcement speech. He did it all already once and with COVID, he is doing it again – rebuilding America. Only Trump.

Trump Escalator Speech snippets:

Wow. Whoa. That is some group of people. Thousands. So nice, thank you very much. That's really nice. Thank you. It's great to be at Trump Tower. It's great to be in a wonderful city, New York. And it's an honor to have everybody here. This is beyond anybody's expectations. There's been no crowd like this.

Our country is in serious trouble. We don't have victories anymore. We used to have victories, but we don't have them. When was the last time anybody saw us beating, let's say, China in a trade deal? They kill us. I beat China all the time. All the time.

When did we beat Japan at anything? They send their cars over by the millions, and what do we do? When was the last time you saw a Chevrolet in Tokyo? It doesn't exist, folks. They beat us all the time.

When do we beat Mexico at the border? They're laughing at us, at our stupidity. And now they are beating us economically. They are not our friend, believe me. But they're killing us economically.

Thank you. It's true, and these are the best and the finest. When Mexico sends its people, they're not sending their best. They're not sending you. They're not sending you. They're sending people that have lots of problems, and they're bringing those problems with us. They're bringing drugs. They're bringing crime. They're rapists. And some, I assume, are good people.

We spent $2 trillion in Iraq, $2 trillion. We lost thousands of lives, thousands in Iraq. We have wounded soldiers, who I love, I love — they're great — all over the place, thousands and thousands of wounded soldiers.

. . .

Our enemies are getting stronger and stronger by the way, and we as a country are getting weaker. Even our nuclear arsenal doesn't work.

It came out recently they have equipment that is 30 years old. They don't know if it worked. And I thought it was horrible when it was broadcast on television, because boy, does that send signals to Putin and all of the other people that look at us and they say, "That is a group of people, and that is a nation that truly has no clue. They don't know what they're doing. They don't know what they're doing."

We have a disaster called the big lie: Obamacare. Obamacare.

And remember the $5 billion website? $5 billion we spent on a website, and to this day it doesn't work. A $5 billion website.

Well, you need somebody, because politicians are all talk, no action. Nothing's gonna get done. They will not bring us— believe me— to the promised land. They will not.

I hear speeches. Fellow Republicans…they don't talk jobs and they don't talk China. When was the last time you heard that China is killing us? They're devaluing their currency to a level that you wouldn't believe. It makes it impossible for our companies to compete, impossible. They're killing us. But you don't hear that from anybody else. You don't hear it from anybody else. And I watch the speeches.

We need— we need somebody— we need somebody that literally will take this country and make it great again. We

can do that. And, I will tell you, I love my life. I have a
wonderful family. They're saying, "Dad, you're going to
do something that's going to be so tough."
I will be the greatest jobs president that God ever created. I
tell you that.

I'll bring back our jobs from China, from Mexico, from
Japan, from so many

I will immediately terminate President Obama's illegal
executive order on immigration, immediately.

Fully support and back up the Second Amendment.
So we have to rebuild our infrastructure, our bridges, our
roadways, our airports. You come into La Guardia
Airport, it's like we're in a third world country. You look at
the patches and the 40-year-old floor. They throw down
asphalt, and they throw.

You look at these airports, we are like a third world
country. And I come in from China and I come in from
Qatar and I come in from different places, and they have
the most incredible airports in the world. You come to back
to this country and you have LAX, disaster. You have all
of these disastrous airports. We have to rebuild our
infrastructure.

Save Medicare, Medicaid and Social Security without cuts.
Have to do it.

Renegotiate our foreign trade deals.

And strengthen our military and take care of our vets. So,
so important.

Sadly, the American dream is dead.

But if I get elected president I will bring it back bigger and better and stronger than ever before, and we will make America great again.

Thank you. Thank you very much.1

So, in this speech, Donald Trump showed that he was no dummy. Furthermore, he spoke American, not politician to the many Americans who had been hearing politician-speak for far too many years. Donald Trump gave this speech and over 300-others like it and his tone never changed. Donald Trump loves America and all Americans who love America love that Donald Trump loves America. That's "Why Donald Trump Got Elected." It is also why he will beat Joe Biden because there is only one Donald Trump and because we need him.

Why did the people vote for Trump?

Americans could not take our country for granted

From the eyes of many, for eight years of Obama running the ship without a license, the United States was in imminent danger and we needed a comprehensive, yet workable solution to bring us back on the right economic track. America needed to be infused with a positive sense of the future so that even before the Tax Reform in December 2017, we would know things were getting so good that we could put the Apply Inside signs back outside.

It's getting better every day. That's "Why Trump Was Elected President!" God helped out a lot but he helped by giving real reasons to vote for Donald Trump and by inspiring Mr. Trump to be himself.

The reason there had been no real middle-class jobs for most of the Obama years, was because the economy was caput. It was not working. Why was it not working? How about not having one businessman on the former president's cabinet to help right the big ship US. It was as if the former president was trying to assure failure.

The prior administration was ideologically driven, and its policies and regulations had made businesses afraid to invest in America. The government was perceived as the chief causative problem for the malaise. Instead of government wanting to help, those in the know, companies were asking for government to please get out of the way.

But, in eight years, the official US would not get out of the way. Instead, it injected itself where it could do the most harm. Some saw their lack of support for America as "that's all she wrote for the country!" Government philosophies had to change for America to have a chance. Donald Trump was perceived as a breath of fresh air. He was what had been missing—a leader who would paint it all fresh with a new paint brush and great paint to boot— the best paint you could get!

One way to change government philosophies of course, would be for the same people, who created the problem, to change their ways. That rarely happens. Another way to change government philosophies is to change governments. We get to do that at the federal level every two to six years with representatives. Once every four years, we get to change Presidents.

This time, the people decided that the presidency should be handed off to the person that had great prospects for success. I speak of Donald J. Trump, who is now our CEO, whether he is liked or un-liked by an unkind press. Americans in 30 of 50 states chose Donald J. Trump and most of us are very pleased that we no longer have to go to a swamp of corruption to hope to move the country forward.

The reason "Why Trump Got Elected!" is because from everything that was out there, only Trump had the guts to fire all the officials who had given up America for Obama. Only Trump could and only Trump wanted to save America for We the People and for those who will live long after us.

I continually thank Mr. Trump for running. He is a tough, brave man. Historians will say that he had lots of other things that he could have done with his time.

Great things sometimes come in email

Like you, I have received many things in email without attribution. Many, I wanted to believe so much that I passed them on without checking anywhere. I do not particularly like Snopes as it almost always, from my observations, gives the liberal socialist progressive viewpoint like as if a Democrat activist did the analysis, and wrote an anti-American thesis about it.

Rarely does Snopes call anything correctly. Things that are very believable are declared false without what I consider a proper explanation. Nonetheless, I use Snopes myself as a conservative Democrat to see what the other side thinks about given matters. Don't count on Snopes for the unbiased truth. In fact, most fact checkers are getting checks from various wings of the Democratic Party for being fine foot soldiers.

By the way, in addition to email, I also found a written piece on https://reclaimourrepublic.wordpress.com. The full URL is https://reclaimourrepublic.wordpress.com/2016/06/02/video-honestly-why-would-anyone-vote-for-trump-press-covers-trump-inaccurately/

Right on the first page of this URL is a picture of this beautiful lady shown for your review on the next page. Just looking at this wonderful picture (seen in color on the Kindle version of this book), would be enough for me to reevaluate my posture on Donald Trump if I did not already know how great he was about to be. And, unlike Obama, a faux great, Trump has proven himself as a great man while on his mission to save America.

My whole extended family and I love the fact that Donald Trump is now our President and we wish him and his family well in this most arduous task. I thank Fred L. Anderson for this great email. It was proudly signed Fred L. Anderson. I could not find it on Snopes, which I believe means that Snopes could find no material to denigrate the piece or the author.

The email is printed on the next pages as received with emphasis asterisks removed. The paragraph immediately below, preceding the email, is from a retired lawyer. I adjusted it very slightly to mute a few words that might first appear objectionable. The essence of what was said is still in the paragraph on the next page.

VIDEO Honestly, Why Would Anyone Vote For Trump? – Press covers Trump inaccurately

Posted on June 2, 2016

Believing fervently that anyone in the phone book would make a better president than either the disgusting creature whom the Dems will nominate or the guy who many liberals think is a narcissistic empty suit, I am trying to see Trump in a better light than that cast by the parrots collectively comprising the national media. I found the attached piece, sent to me by a Naples, Florida, retiree, encouraging in that regard, and would commend it to your attention.

Here is the rest of the Email/Article:

Honestly, Why you should vote for Trump? – Press covers Trump inaccurately

A few days ago someone -- I don't know who, asked this question … and a mutual friend (knowing I am a Trump supporter), tagged me and asked me to answer the question. Here is my reply from during the heat of the campaign. Email Reply from Fred L. Anderson:

[This is an answer to "Why Trump Got Elected!"]

I am a Trump supporter for several reasons. I believe that our country is at a critical tipping point and we don't have another presidential term to figure this out.

Health care costs are out of control, our labor participation rate is at a 50-year low, we have no borders, jobs are leaving by the thousands, the debt service on our national debt is nearing a point where we simply cannot pay it.

The average person hasn't had an increase in pay in 12 years. Over half the black men in our country are out of work. We are more divided than I can ever remember and I'm over 60 years old. We are at the brink of losing our country.

On top of that we spend money we don't have fighting wars we shouldn't be in, and cannot win. We pay over a hundred other countries billions of dollars a year and our military are the policemen for the world. We must fix this mess ASAP.

Now, before I give you my reasons, I need to share my perspective. I am an evangelical Christian. but I don't believe it is the role of government to legislate morality. I am a service connected disabled veteran having served in the US Army as a paratrooper.

I started my second career as an auto mechanic and worked my way up to owning 12 auto repair franchises. I then sold them and began a new career in real estate, building my own company to over 150 agents.

Then in 2003 I invented a technology that put me on CNN and I began selling that software to real estate agents internationally. I've written 14 books, thousands of trade articles and have trained over 1,000,000 real estate agents in specific professional skills.

I've employed over a thousand people during that time, and until a month ago have been a registered democrat. Okay, now that you know where I'm coming from, here are my reasons:

First, his resume. Of everyone running for president, Trump is the only one who has ever employed anyone. He is the only one who has any experience in international trade. He is the only one who understands the impact of our tax laws and government regulation on companies and jobs.

Trump has made a fortune turning around failed companies. He's worked complicated deals all over the world, negotiating with governments, labor unions, and international financiers. These skills are not learned overnight and we don't have time for another life-long politician and attorney to get up to speed.

Second is his character. He is tough as nails. His children are pretty awesome. You can tell a lot about somebody by their kids. He is brutally honest as opposed to being politically correct. His employees and his ex-employees have nothing but praise for him. Even his ex-wives have nothing bad to say about him. Check it out.

Third is his success. He has built hundreds of successful businesses. One of his companies declared bankruptcy (chapter 11 or reorganization) four separate times before ultimately saving the company. All creditors were paid, and jobs were saved. Bottom line is he is just a very good businessman.

Fourth is that he is a great negotiator. In fact, he wrote the book on negotiation -- The Art of the Deal, an international best-seller. If we are to save this country, we need someone who can work with people of differing opinions. Congress is grid locked. We need to work new trade agreements with other nations. We need to renegotiate treaties.

Fifth, Trump is a nationalist and not a globalist. He believes that our country comes first. We need to enforce our borders and the rule of law. He believes it is not our job to defend the whole world. He believes that if we do help countries with their defense, we should be paid for it.

Sixth, he has great instincts. He predicted the rise of Osama bin Laden. He predicted a terror attack on a major US city. He opposed the war in Iraq although every other candidate, but Bernie Sanders was in favor of the war. He opposed it because it would destabilize the Middle East. He got out of the gaming industry before it crashed. Great instincts.

Seventh, he is a natural leader. Even those who don't like him are following his lead. He has single-handedly set the agenda for this election cycle. He is respected internationally as well as in our nation. He oozes leadership.

Eighth, he is a great communicator and persuader. He is a master at using the media to advance his narrative. He totally understands the media. He built the most successful reality show in the history of television. These are skills he will need if he is to turn this country around.

Ninth, I have studied him. I read his first book in 1987 and realized he was a brilliant businessman. I've watched hundreds of hours of speeches, media interviews, read thousands of articles about him, several of his books, and studied his successes and his failures. He is the real deal. I challenge anyone to study him and not support him.

Finally, I have to look at what motivates him. Most politicians are motivated by money and/or power. Trump already has both. He has a history of being a patriot, from his military high school, to now. He has a huge ego, like every other candidate running. The difference is he is honest about his.

I think he sees our nation at a critical place and he knows that he has the unique skill set to fix the problems. If he does, he will go down in history as being one of the greatest presidents ever.

If you understand him, you know that his legacy is important to him (his name on all his buildings and companies). I even believe he is funding his own campaign, so he won't owe favors or loyalties to special interests. When you evaluate his motivations, you can't help but admire him.

I remembered one more reason. Everyone is about to blow a gasket over him. The establishment Republican Party hates him and has actually been actively trying to take down their own front runner. The establishment Democrat Party hates him because they know he will crush Hillary in the election, and the establishment media hates him because he totally controls the news cycle and they cannot control him. Even the donor class hates him because he cannot be bought. If all these people who I cannot stand, hate him, that only makes me love him more.

You know who loves him? The regular people in this country. The ones who work their asses off every day and haven't had a pay raise in over a decade. The ones who pay the taxes and watch as their jobs get shipped overseas or across the border. The ones who see their property values going down because corrupt Big Banking blew up the housing market. The ones whose retirement is in jeopardy because social security has been raided and their 401Ks have been decimated by corrupt Wall Street.

Think about this: We've had politicians running our country for way too many years and look at the results. Isn't it time we give a business person the opportunity to show the way a country should be run.....like a business, because that's what our country is!*

Fred L Anderson

-----Fred, this is Brian, also in my sixties at this time... I agree... Thank you for writing this to all of America!

Thank you for choosing this book to help you better understand why the people love Donald J. Trump and

"Why God helped Trump Get Elected!"

It still is a great feeling, is it not?

Other Books by Brian W. Kelly: (amazon.com, and Kindle)

COVID-19 Mask, Yes? Or No? It's Everybody's Recommended Solution!!!
LSU Tigers Championship Seasons Starts at beginning of LSU Football to the National Championship
Great Coaches in LSU Football Book starts with the first LSU coach; goes to Orgeron Championship
Great Players in LSU Football Begins with 1893 QB Ruffin G Pleasant to 2019 QB Burrow
America for Millennialsl A growing # of disintegrationists want to tear US down
Great Moments in LSU Football Book starts at start of Football to the Ed Orgeron Championship.
The Constitution's Role in a Return to Normalcy Can the Constitution Survive?
The Constitution vs. The Virus Simultaneous attack coronavirus and US governors
One, Two, Three, Pooph!!! Reopen Country Now! Return to normalcy is just around the corner.
Reopen America Now Return to Normalcy
Enough is Enough!Re Re: Covid, We are not children. We're adults.We'll make the right decisions.
How to Write Your 1st Book & Publish it Using Amazon KDP You can do it
REMDESIVIR A Ray of Hope
When Will America Reopen for Business? This author's opinion includes voices of experts
HydroxyChloroquine: The Game Changer
Super Bowl & NFL Championship Seasons The KC Chiefs From the 1st to Super Bowl LIV
Great Coaches in Kansas City Chiefs Football First Coach era to Andy Reid Era
Great Players in Kansas City Chiefs Football From the AFL to Andy Reid Era
Reopen America Now! How to Shut-Down Corona Virus & Return to Normalcy!
Why is Everybody Moving to the Villages? You can afford a home in the Villages
CORONAVIRUS The Cause & the Cure. Many solutions—but which ones will work?
Great Moments in Kansas City Chiefs Football. From the beginning to the Andy Reid Era
How the Philadelphia Eagles Lost Its Karma. This is the one place that tells the story
Cancel All Student Debt Now! Good for America, Good for the Economy.
Social Security Screw Job!!! Scandal: Seniors Intentionally Screwed by US Government
Trump Hate They hate Trump Supporters; Trump; & God—in that order
Christmas Wings for Brian A heartwarming story of a boy whose shoulders kept growing
Merry Christmas to Wilkes-Barre 50 Ways" for Mayor George Brown to Create a Better City.
Air Force Football Championship Seasons From AF Championship to Coach Calhoun's latest team
Syracuse Football Championship Seasons beginning of SU championships; goes to Dino Babers Era
Navy Football Championship Seasons 1st Navy Championships to the Ken Niumatalolo Era
Army Football Championship Seasons Beginning of Football championships to Jeff Monken Era
Florida Gators Championship Seasons Beginning of Football through championships to Dan Mullen era
Alabama's Championship Seasons Beginning of Football past the 2017/2018 National Championship
Clemson Tigers Championship Seasons Beginning of Football to the Clemson National Championships
Penn State's Championship Seasons PSU's first championship to the James Franklin era
Notre Dame's Championship Seasons Before Knute Rockne and past Lou Holtz's 1988 undisputed title
Super Bowls & Championship Seasons: The New York Giants Many championships of the Giants.
Super Bowls & Championship Seasons: New England Patriots Many championships of the Patriots.
Super Bowls & Championship Seasons: The Pittsburgh Steelers Many championship of the Steelers.
Super Bowls & Championship Seasons: The Philadelphia Eagles Many championships of the Eagles.
The Big Toxic School Wilkes-Barre Area's Tale of Corruption, Deception, Taxation & Tyranny
Great Players in New York Giants Football Begins with great players of 1925 to the Saquon Barqley era.
Great Coaches in New York Giants Football Begins with Bob Folwell 1925 and to Pat Shurmur in 2019.
Great Moments in New York Giants Football Beginning of Football to the Pat Shurmur era.
Hasta La Vista California Give California its independence.
IT's ALL OVER! Mueller: "NO COLLUSION!"—Top Dems going to jail for the hoax!
Democrat Secret for Power & Winning Elections Open borders adds millions of new Democrat Voters
Hope for Wilkes-Barre—John Q. Doe—Next Mayor of Wilkes-Barre
The John Doe Plan & WB Plan will help create a better city!
Great Moments in New England Patriots Football Second Edition
This book begins at the beginning of Football and goes to the Bill Belichick era.
The Cowardly Congress Corrupt US Congress is against America and Americans.
Great Players in Air Force Football From the beginning to the current season
Great Coaches in Air Force Football Grom the beginning to Coach Troy Calhoun
Help for Mayor George and Next Mayor of Wilkes-Barre How to vote for the next Mayor Council
Ghost of Wilkes-Barre Future: Spirit's advice for residents how to pick the next Mayor and Council
Great Players in Air Force Football: Air Force's best players of all time
Great Coaches in Air Force Football: From Coach 1 to Coach Troy Calhoun
Great Moments in Air Force Football: From day 1 to today

Great Players in Navy Football: Navy's best including Bellino & Staubach
Great Coaches in Navy Football: From Coach 1 to Coach #39 Ken Niumatalolo
Great Moments in Navy Football: From day 1 to coach Ken Niumatalolo 1
No Tree! No Toys! No Toot! Heartwarming story. Christmas gone while 19 month old napped
How to End DACA, Sanctuary Cities, & Resident Illegal Aliens . best solution remove shadowsAmerica.
Government Must Stop Ripping Off Seniors' Social Security!: Hey buddy, seniors can't spare a dime?
Special Report: Solving America's Student Debt Crisis!: The only real solution to the $1.52 Trillion debt
The Winning Political Platform for America Unique winning approach to solve big problems in America.
Lou Barletta v Bob Casey for US Senate Barletta's unique approach to solve big problems in America.
John Chrin v Matt Cartwright for Congress Chrin has a unique approach to solve big problems in America.
The Cure for Hate !!! Can the cure be any worse than this disease that is crippling America?
Andrew Cuomo's Time to Go? "He Was Never that Great!"**:** Cuomo says America never that great
White People Are Bad! Bad! Bad! Whoever thought a popular slogan in 2018 *It's OK to be White!*
The Fake News Media Is Also Corrupt !!!: Fake press / media today is not worthy to be 4th Estate.
God Gave US Donald Trump? Trump was sent from God as the people's answer
Millennials Say America Was "Never That Great": Too many pleased days of political chumps not over!
It's Time for The John Q. Doe Party… Don't you think? By Elephants.
Great Players in Florida Gators Football… Tim Tebow and a ton of other great players
Great Coaches in Florida Gators Football… The best coaches in Gator history.
The Constitution by Hamilton, Jefferson, Madison, et al. The Real Constitution
The Constitution Companion. Will help you learn and understand the Constitution
Great Coaches in Clemson Football The best Clemson Coaches right to Dabo Swinney
Great Players in Clemson Football The best Clemson players in history
Winning Back America. America's been stolen and can be won back completely
The Founding of America… Great book to pick up a lot of great facts
Defeating America's Career Politicians. The scoundrels need to go.
Midnight Mass by Jack Lammers… You remember what it was like Great story
The Bike by Jack Lammers… Great heartwarming Story by Jack
Wipe Out All Student Loan Debt--Now! Watch the economy go boom!
No Free Lunch Pay Back Welfare! Why not pay it back?
Deport All Millennials Now!!! Why they deserve to be deported and/or saved
DELETE the EPA, Please! The worst decisions to hurt America
Taxation Without Representation 4th Edition Should we throw the TEA overboard again?
Four Great Political Essays by Thomas Dawson
Top Ten Political Books for 2018… Cliffnotes Version of 10 Political Books
Top Six Patriotic Books for 2018… Cliffnotes version of 6 Patriotic Boosk
Why Trump Got Elected!.. It's great to hear about a great milestone in America!
The Day the Free Press Died. Corrupt Press Lives on!
Solved (Immigration) The best solutions for 2018
Solved II (Obamacare, Social Security, Student Debt) Check it out; They're solved.
Great Moments in Pittsburgh Steelers Football... Six Super Bowls and more.
Great Players in Pittsburgh Steelers Football ,,,Chuck Noll, Bill Cowher, Mike Tomin, etc.
Great Coaches in New England Patriots Football,,, Bill Belichick the one and only plus others
Great Players in New England Patriots Football… Tom Brady, Drew Bledsoe et al.
Great Coaches in Philadelphia Eagles Football..Andy Reid, Doug Pederson & Lots more
Great Players in Philadelphia Eagles Football Great players such as Sonny Jurgenson
Great Coaches in Syracuse Football All the greats including Ben Schwartzwalder
Great Players in Syracuse Football. Highlights best players such as Jim Brown & Donovan McNabb
Millennials are People Too !!! Give US millennials help to live American Dream
Brian Kelly for the United States Senate from PA: Fresh Face for US Senate
The Candidate's Bible. Don't pray for your campaign without this bible
Rush Limbaugh's Platform for Americans… Rush will love it
Sean Hannity's Platform for Americans… Sean will love it
Donald Trump's New Platform for Americans. Make Trump unbeatable in 2020
Tariffs Are Good for America! One of the best tools a president can have
Great Coaches in Pittsburgh Steelers Football Sixteen of the best coaches ever to coach in pro football.
Great Moments in New England Patriots Football Great football moments from Boston to New England
Great Moments in Philadelphia Eagles Football. The best from the Eagles from the beginning of football.
Great Moments in Syracuse Football The great moments, coaches & players in Syracuse Football
Boost Social Security Now! Hey Buddy Can You Spare a Dime?
The Birth of American Football. From the first college game in 1869 to the last Super Bowl
Obamacare: A One-Line Repeal Congress must get this done.
A Wilkes-Barre Christmas Story A wonderful town makes Christmas all the better
A Boy, A Bike, A Train, and a Christmas Miracle A Christmas story that will melt your heart

Pay-to-Go   America-First Immigration Fix
Legalizing Illegal Aliens Via Resident Visas Americans-first plan saves $Trillions. Learn how!
60 Million Illegal Aliens in America!!! A simple, America-first solution.
The Bill of Rights By Founder James Madison Refresh *your knowledge of the specific rights for all*
Great Players in Army Football Great Army Football played by great players..
Great Coaches in Army Football Army's coaches are all great.
Great Moments in Army Football Army Football at its best.
Great Moments in Florida Gators Football Gators Football from the start. This is the book.
Great Moments in Clemson Football CU Football at its best. This is the book.
Great Moments in Florida Gators Football Gators Football from the start. This is the book.
The Constitution Companion. A Guide to Reading and Comprehending the Constitution
The Constitution by Hamilton, Jefferson, & Madison – Big type and in English
PATERNO: The Dark Days After Win # 409. Sky began to fall within days of win # 409.
JoePa 409 Victories: Say No More! Winningest Division I-A football coach ever
American College Football: The Beginning From before day one football was played.
Great Coaches in Alabama Football Challenging the coaches of every other program!
Great Coaches in Penn State Football the Best Coaches in PSU's football program
Great Players in Penn State Football The best players in PSU's football program
Great Players in Notre Dame Football The best players in ND's football program
Great Coaches in Notre Dame Football The best coaches in any football program
Great Players in Alabama Football from Quarterbacks to offensive Linemen Greats!
Great Moments in Alabama Football AU Football from the start. This is the book.
Great Moments in Penn State Football PSU Football, start--games, coaches, players,
Great Moments in Notre Dame Football ND Football, start, games, coaches, players
Cross Country with the Parents A great trip from East Coast to West with the kids
Seniors, Social Security & the Minimum Wage. Things seniors need to know.
How to Write Your First Book and Publish It with CreateSpace. You too can be an author.
The US Immigration Fix--It's all in here. Finally, an answer.
I had a Dream IBM Could be #1 Again The title is self-explanatory
WineDiets.Com Presents The Wine Diet Learn how to lose weight while having fun.
Wilkes-Barre, PA; Return to Glory Wilkes-Barre City's return to glory
Geoffrey Parsons' Epoch... The Land of Fair Play Better than the original.
The Bill of Rights 4 Dummmies! This is the best book to learn about your rights.
Sol Bloom's Epoch ...Story of the Constitution The best book to learn the Constitution
America 4 Dummmies! All Americans should read to learn about this great country.
The Electoral College 4 Dummmies! How does it really work?
The All-Everything Machine Story about IBM's finest computer server.
ThankYou IBM! This book explains how IBM was beaten in the computer marketplace by neophytes

Amazon.com/author/brianwkelly
Brian W. Kelly has written 224 books including this one.
Thank you for buying this one.
Others can be found at amazon.com/author/brianwkelly